Clergy Response
to Suicidal Persons
and Their Family Members

Clergy Response to Suicidal Persons and Their Family Members

An Interfaith Resource Book for Clergy and Congregations

Edited by

David C. Clark, Ph.D.
Center for Suicide Research and Prevention
Rush Institute for Mental Well-Being
Rush-Presbyterian-St. Luke's Medical Center

Exploration Press
Chicago, Illinois

Studies in Ministry and Parish Life

Exploration Press
Chicago Theological Seminary
5757 University Avenue
Chicago, Illinois 60637

ISBN: Cloth-0-913552-49-6
　　　 Paper: 0-913552-50-x

Library of Congress Catalog Card Number: 93-72090

The mind is its own place, and in itself
Can make a heav'n of hell, a hell of heav'n.
        John Milton
        Paradise Lost (1667)

But what is God saying through a good man's suicide?... To try to
express in even the most insightful and theologically sophisticat-
ed terms the meaning of what God speaks through the events of
our lives is as precarious a business as to try to express the meaning of the sound of rain on the roof or the spectacle of the setting
sun. But I choose to believe that he speaks nonetheless, and the
reason that his words are impossible to capture in human language is of course that they are ultimately always incarnate
words. They are words fleshed out in the everydayness no less
than in the crises of our own experience.
        Frederick Buechner
        The Sacred Journey (1982)

... and began to think that her prospects might be brightening,
and that better days might be dawning upon them. Such is hope,
Heaven's own gift to struggling mortals; pervading, like some
subtle essence, from the skies, all things, both good and bad; as
universal as death, and more infectious than disease.
        Charles Dickens
        The Life and Adventures of Nicholas Nickleby (1839)

Table of Contents

Preface

The Clergy Advisory Committee of the Center for Suicide Research and Prevention at Rush-Presbyterian-St. Luke's Medical Center in Chicago began to meet in 1986 to explore ways to translate the practical implications of current suicide research findings for the benefit of clergy with congregations. While in the last decade seminaries have tended to offer some training in counseling and psychopathology to their clergy candidates, many senior clergy with congregations completed their studies in an era when less curricular attention was devoted to mental health issues — and when mental health professionals understood a great deal less about suicide than they do now. Even for those exposed to classes in crisis intervention and psychopathology, the death by suicide of a congregant or the family member of a congregant imposes urgent demands for a clerical response for which one may not be prepared. To address these concerns, the Clergy Advisory Group (a mix of clergy with congregations, pastoral counselors, and seminary faculty) organized a series of conferences on "Clergy Response to Suicidal Persons and Their Family Members." The enthusiastic response convinced us of the need for more continuing education activities of this type. This book is our third undertaking.

We owe a debt of gratitude to two organizations and a number of individuals, without whom this project would never have been realized. The Clergy Advisory Committee of the Center for Suicide Research and Prevention was the launching pad for this project. The Arthur Rubloff Institute for Jewish Living at Temple Sholom in Chicago was the booster rocket, insofar as the Rubloff Institute embraced, funded, and hosted the conference that served as the basis for this book.

The faculty, mental health professionals, and research scientists working within the **Center for Suicide Research and Prevention at Rush-Presbyterian-St. Luke's Medical Center in Chicago** share a mission to prevent suicide and self-harm by persons of all ages. By helping to develop a better scientific understanding of the causes of suicide, those of us engaged in clinical research hope to identify more effective treatment and prevention measures with the potential to reduce death and injury. Center staff members assess and treat patients who are suicidal or who have attempted suicide, provide support services to family members of persons who have attempted or died by suicide, and work to increase public awareness that suicide is preventable.

The Arthur Rubloff Institute for Jewish Living was established at Temple Sholom in Chicago, Illinois to honor the wishes of the late Arthur Rubloff. The Institute is devoted to making available the best of current Jewish thought and activity, and to enlarging the possibilities for effective and meaningful living in today's world. We would like to thank the Arthur Rubloff Institute Committee, its Rabbinic Advisor Rabbi Steven Denker, the Temple Sholom Board of Directors, and Dr. Ira Halper, a director of Temple Sholom, for their confidence and support.

Five individuals deserve special mention because without their ideas and encouragement, there would be no book. Four are represented by chapters in this volume: Father Charles Rubey, Rabbi Robert Marx, Dr. George Fitchett, and Rev. Dan Stauffacher. The fifth individual we want to acknowledge is Rev. David Whitermore, formerly director of the Church Federation of Greater Chicago. He showed faith and confidence in our earliest plans, and unstintingly shared his experience in planning interfaith projects. We are fortunate to have friends such as these.

Clergy Response
to Suicidal Persons
and Their Family Members

I. Introduction

David C. Clark, Ph.D.

Suicide is the *eighth* leading cause of death in the United States. This fact makes it evident that suicide is a *major public health problem*. Suicide is an equal-opportunity tragedy — it touches every age group, race, ethnic group, and social class. National survey data shows that three percent of living adults have tried to kill themselves and nine percent admit to having had suicidal thoughts during the past year. One of every hundred persons dies by suicide. The suicidal behavior of a family member profoundly affects the lives of 3,800,000 Americans each year.

Deaths by suicide are almost invariably associated with psychiatric illness. But 80% of persons who die by suicide were not being treated for their psychiatric illness in the months preceding death, and half had never seen a mental health professional in their entire lifetimes. Why do the psychiatric illnesses that play such an important role in suicidal behavior go unrecognized and untreated? The two principal culprits are *ignorance* and *fear of stigma*. Many people don't know how to recognize major psychiatric illness — and when they do recognize a psychiatric illness in themselves or in a family member, they are often reluctant to talk about the matter for fear they will be "branded."

An essential ingredient of all suicide prevention activities should be the lesson that psychiatric illnesses are as "real" as diabetes or a bone fracture. Eight percent of the U.S. population experiences at least one episode of serious mood disorder in their lifetime, and 13% abuse alcohol at some point in their life. At any given point in time, two percent of the population are suffering with major depression and three percent are abusing alcohol (Regier et al., 1988). These two illnesses — major depression and alcoholism — are implicated as contributing factors in more than two-thirds of all deaths by suicide (Clark & Horton-Deutsch, 1992).

Effective treatments are widely available, but only a third of persons suffering with a psychiatric illness seek professional treatment. A recent multi-hospital treatment study pitting a standard antidepressant medication against two types of depression-specific short-term psychotherapies showed that 70% of depressed outpatients responded well to either the active drug or psychotherapy conditions (Elkin et al., 1989). Alcoholism treatment programs and Alcoholics Anonymous return many (not all) to a sober lifestyle.

The men and women of the clergy can be pivotal resources for combating mental illness in general and suicide in particular. The clergy are integral members of the communities in which they live and work. They are spiritual leaders and counselors of first resort within their congregations. A recent national study of mental health and help-seeking showed that persons with *serious* psychiatric disorders were just as likely to seek help from clergy as from mental health professionals — and half of the seriously ill persons who consulted clergy never made any contacts with a mental health professional. (Larson et al., 1988). A recent Gallup Organization survey (1992) demonstrated that older adults are more willing to turn to their clergy than to physicians and psychiatrists for help when someone they know is considering suicide. Simply put, many people feel more comfortable taking their personal problems to their own minister, priest, or rabbi than to their family doctor or local mental health professional.

The tragedies of suicide attempts and death by suicide can often be averted if prevailing mental disorders are promptly recognized and treated — even when the aversive life circumstances of the patient cannot be changed one iota. The pastor who brings a holistic approach to persons in crisis is in a unique position to distinguish between spiritual trials, difficult life circumstances, psychological idiosyncrasies, relationship problems, normal grieving, and frank psychiatric illness. These are not easy distinctions for anyone to make. Many persons in crisis struggle with a number of different problems simultaneously. Sometimes the boundaries between different types of problems are blurred. The vigilant pastor who has been taught to recognize fundamental signs of psychiatric illness, however, is in a strategic position to spot persons struggling with a mental disorder, educate them about the nature of mental disorders, dispel some of the stigma attached to mental disorders, and vigorously encourage consultation with a qualified mental health professional.

This book consists of a series of pastoral perspectives on suicide-related problems and the opportunities they pose for pastoral ministry. Each chapter represents a wealth of individual and congregational experiences on the frontier between spiritual ministry and mental health care. Faith equips each of us with a number of tools that always stand us in good stead when responding to a suicidal crisis — including (in the words of Charles Dickens), "... hope, Heaven's own gift to struggling mortals."

References

Clark DC, Horton-Deutsch SL: Assessment *in absentia*: The value of the psychological autopsy method for studying antecedents of suicide and predicting future suicides. In Maris RL, Berman A, Maltsberger JT, Yufit RY (editors): *Assessment and Prediction of Suicide*. New York, Guilford Press, 1992, pages 144-182.

Elkin I, Shea MT, Watkins JT, Imber SD, Sotsky SM, Collins JF, Glass DR, Pilkonis PA, Leber WR, Docherty JP, Fiester SJ, Parloff MB: National Institute of Mental Health Treatment of Depression Collaborative Research Program: General effectiveness of treatments. *Archives of General Psychiatry* 46: 971-982, 1989.

Gallup Organization: Attitude and Incidence of Suicide Among the Elderly. Princeton, New Jersey, The Gallup Organization, Inc., 1992.

Larson DB, Hohmann AA, Kessler LG, Meador KG, Boyd JH, McSherry E: The couch and the cloth: The need for linkage. *Hospital and Community Psychiatry* 39: 1064-1069, 1988.

Regier DA, Boyd JH, Burke JD, Rae DS, Myers JK, Kramer M, Robins LN, George LK, Karno M, Locke BZ: One-month prevalence of mental disorders in the United States: Based on five epidemiologic catchment area sites. *Archives of General Psychiatry* 45: 977-986, 1988.

II. Suicide in Theological Traditions

Introduction

Historically, religious leaders and civil authorities of Western civilization tended to condemn suicide as both a sin and a crime. Today, what positions do Jewish, Catholic, and Protestant theologians take on the matter of suicide? It is particularly valuable to consider all three theological commentaries that follow as a group, because: (a) there is a remarkable degree of consensus among all three, and (b) there is a widespread inclination for people to assume that while *their* religious tradition has "enlightened, modern" views about suicide, *other* traditions labor under the influence of antiquated facts and generally fail to consider the psychological plight of the bereaved.

In what follows, Rabbi Denker explains why Jewish Law interprets most suicides as irrational acts committed by persons who should not to be held responsible for their actions. In a similar vein, Dr. Gallagher shows that according to Catholic teachings, one should assume the presence of "an acute mental disturbance" rather than judge the subjective guilt of anyone who takes his/her own life. Dr. Anderson outlines a set of five theological propositions about life, death, and faith grounded in Protestant theology — propositions that underline why pastors are called upon to offer a full ministry of care to the families of suicide victims. All three religious traditions agree that the families of suicide victims should not be denied the traditional mourning rituals intended for the well-being of the living.

For further background on how acts of suicide and martyrdom were treated in ancient and classical theological literature, the reader may be interested to refer to the book *A Noble Death: Suicide and Martyrdom Among Christians and Jews in Antiquity* by Arthur Droge and James Tabor (Harper-Collins, 1992).

Chapter 1

Suicide in the Hebrew Bible and the Rabbinic Tradition

Rabbi Steven L. Denker

Introduction

The Hebrew Bible[1] and its interpretation through the Rabbinic Tradition[2] form the basis for Judaism's understanding of and approach to the critical issues of life. Suicide is no exception. The purpose of this chapter is to provide the reader with a brief description of the occurrences of and attitudes toward suicide that are expressed in the Hebrew Scripture and developed by the rabbis. Although by no means exhaustive, this chapter relies on many classical and secondary sources. It is an examination of suicide intended for the reader who requires a ready reference to the Jewish perspective on this subject. The student needing greater detail is well advised to refer to the bibliography and the classical sources cited herein. Also, by its nature, this article cannot provide an authoritative response to any specific suicide. Questions regarding the proper Jewish approach to any particular incident should be directed to a rabbi.

This article is written from the unique perspective of the Jewish understanding of God's will and the nature of human life. Judaism is open to all who want to partake of its wisdom but does not contend that the Jewish way is the *only* way. Therefore, nothing in this article should be deemed as polemic or as an attempt to argue against any other system of belief or perception of the Divine Will.

The Rabbinic Tradition focuses on the needs of the living and separates its response to suicide into two areas of concern. In one, the attitude toward the victim or person who attempted suicide must be examined. Here the question of the suicide completer as possible transgressor of the Divine Law is at issue. Allied to this is society's need to discourage the unnecessary taking of life — including one's own. The second area of concern, perhaps unique in Jewish Tradition, is the separation of the needs of the mourners from the question of the culpability of the suicide victim. Clergy and others who care for the mourners of suicide victims will be particularly interested in this aspect of Jewish Law.

Finally, this consideration of suicide in the Rabbinic Tradition excludes the clouded cases of supposed martyrdom and execution as a punishment for criminal activity. The Rabbinic Tradition discusses situations in which one may (but is not required) accept death in Sanctification of God's Name.[3] It also concludes that the knowing perpetrator of a capital crime has forfeited his or her life as a willful suicide.[4] Martyrdom is of questionable value and certainly not encouraged by mainstream Jewish thinking. Criminal activity is condemned by Judaism; however, under the Rabbinic Tradition capital punishment is almost impossible to carry out. While death through both martyrdom and execution can both be reasonably discussed as forms of suicide, they raise theological, ethical, and public policy issues that go well beyond the scope of this article. Therefore, our discussion will be limited to cases that do not involve either of these factors.

Suicide in the Hebrew Bible

Suicide is a rare phenomenon in the Hebrew Bible. There is no term for suicide in Biblical Hebrew and no occurrence of self-inflicted death in the first six books of the Bible. The few biblical incidents of suicide occur in connection with other issues, always under stress, as a means of avoiding ignominious military defeat and/or postmortem disgrace, and sometimes as a punishment from God. The question of whether or not the suicide victim is held culpable and punished in the afterlife does not arise. The Hebrew Bible contains no notion of reward and punishment in an afterlife, but knows only of *sheol*, a place where all deceased go.

Rather than a reward or punishment in a speculative afterlife, the Hebrew Bible views the cutting short of earthly life as a punishment in itself.

The first occurrences of apparent suicide take place in the Book of Judges. Abimelech, a son of Jerubbaal, ruler of the Northern Kingdom and briefly the ruler of the city of Shechem, was hit by an upper millstone thrown down by a woman defender as he attacked the fortified tower at Thebez. Wounded, Abimelech asked his arms bearer to "finish me off" so as to avoid the disgrace of being killed by a woman. The text clearly states that his death is Divine Retribution for evil he had done. Presumably, both the defender of the tower and the arms bearer are instruments of God's justice. The arms bearer's complicity in Abimelech's death is not discussed.[5] A reaction to assisted suicide must wait for the Second Book of Samuel.

The death of Samson is not clearly a suicide.[6] Blinded and humiliated, the imprisoned Samson is the object of Philistine scorn. Samson's prayer for the return of his fabled strength seems to be answered when he said that he would just as soon die with the Philistines. However, there is no clear statement that he intends to die — only that he would do so if it would end his torment and destroy his tormentors.[7] Samson's death could be described as an unfortunate miscalculation. The text, for no apparent reason, mentions that his hair was growing back — perhaps along with his strength? Regardless of whether Samson's death was a suicide or simply an heroic act to liberate his people, it remains clear that his death was an attempt to end his humiliation. Further, stating only that Samson was buried in his father's tomb after having ruled Israel for twenty years, the Bible does not consider Samson's death to be a disgrace.

Two versions of the death of King Saul occur at the end of I Samuel and the beginning of II Samuel.[8] Defeated by the Philistines at Mount Gilboa, his sons already dead and wounded himself, Saul seeks to end his own life before his enemies can make sport of him. In the first telling Saul, like Abimelech, asks his arms bearer to assist in his death. In awe the servant refuses and Saul takes his own life. Seeing the King dead, the unnamed arms bearer takes his own life. The Philistines, as Saul expected, disgraced and dishonored his body. In the second recension, word of Saul's death reaches David through an Amalekite who claims to have assisted in Saul's death. In agony, Saul requested assistance in dying. Knowing that Saul would never recover, the Amalakite complied. David, who clearly disapproved of this act, ordered the Amalakite executed.

Here, the Bible repeats the motif of a suicide committed in the face of certain death and done to avoid the disgrace of falling into the hands of one's enemy. Saul, under duress, is not held accountable for his actions. Assisted suicide is a new element introduced in the account of King Saul's death. In both variant reports, the Biblical text does not condemn Saul for his actions but clearly argues against assisting in another's suicide. First, in awe (presumably of God) the Israelite arms-bearer declines to assist even at the request of his King. Second, the pagan appears before a disapproving David unashamed of his act and is punished.

Suicide to avoid the shame of defeat appears in two other Biblical narratives. Ahithophel, an advisor to King David who became a traitor and joined Absalom's rebellion, fell out of favor with the would-be king and hung himself. Even though his suicide seems to have been premeditated, Ahithophel is not disgraced in death. Like Samson, he is buried honorably in his ancestral tomb. Zimri,[9] who fails to hold power after his assassination of King Elah and the members of the royal household of Baasha of the Northern Kingdom, ended his seven-day reign besieged in the citadel of the palace. Zimri set the citadel afire and died in the blaze. The text explicitly attributes his death to the sins he had committed in rebelling against Elah and murdering the King and the royal household.[10]

Against the backdrop of the entire Hebrew Bible, accounts of suicide are sparse. However, we can draw some conclusions from the common elements that do appear. The clear suicides are all committed in the face of disastrous defeat and humiliation (before and/or after death). In addition, mortal injury, great pain and sin are sometimes factors. Assisted suicide, in the one case where it is addressed, is twice condemned, once by the inaction of Saul's arms-bearer and again by David's execution of the Amalekite. Even though death itself may constitute punishment, one who has committed suicide under any of these circumstances is neither punished nor denied burial for having taken his own life.

With this background, the stage is set to examine the development of the Rabbinic Tradition's tenet that one who commits suicide under conditions of great mental or physical stress is not responsible for his actions and is not accountable for the transgression of suicide.

The Rabbinic tradition

The term in Rabbinic Hebrew for suicide is *abed et atzmo*,[11] literally the one who "loses himself." The root of *abed* is the same as the root used in the phrase "My father was a *lost* Aramean."[12] In light of the fact that other verbs and expressions meaning to "kill," "murder" or "spill blood" are readily available in the Hebrew language, the chosen, softer usage connotes the treatment given suicide in the Rabbinic Tradition. The thrust of the law is to find the suicide unintentional. Even in the rare instance when a suicide is deemed intentional, the family is treated as any other group of mourners.[13]

The Rabbinic attitude toward suicide is that it is a prohibited shedding of blood. This is made clear in the Midrash, Genesis Rabbah and in the Mishneh Torah, Maimonides' law code.[14] The suicide is to be denied full burial rites and some authorities believe that the suicide is denied life in the hereafter. However, as with any other crime, Jewish Law finds culpable only those who transgress the law knowingly, willfully, and without duress. Suicide is no exception to this aspect of Jewish Law.

To make a finding of willful suicide in the Rabbinic Tradition the strict standard of proof first enunciated in the post-Talmudic tractate Semahot must be met:

> Who [is in the category] of willful suicide? Not he who [only] climbed to the top of a tree and fell and died or who [only] went to the top of a roof and fell and died. Rather, it is he who [first and in the presence of witnesses] cried out, "Look, I am going to the tip of the roof or the top of the tree and I will throw myself down that I may die." and people saw him go up to the top of the tree or roof and he fell and died.[15]

Later authorities raise the level of proof even higher by specifying that the victim must immediately be observed ascending to the same roof in an angry or agitated manner. The fatal fall must immediately follow the declaration.[16] A threat, followed by a fatal fall days or even hours later, could not be presumed a suicide. This combined with the understanding that life-saving overrides almost all other obligations under Jewish Law, makes a finding of a willful suicide all but impossible. The tractate continues by specifying that a person found dead, even under circumstances that may suggest suicide, is presumed not to have committed suicide willfully.

The 16th century law code, Shulchan Aruch, adds a blanket exemption from willful suicide for minors as well as adults who knew what they were doing, made a statement, but were "trapped." King Saul is specifically mentioned in this context.[17]

In the modern practice of Judaism this means that rarely are burial rites denied even if there is a finding of suicide under civil law. It is, therefore, possible to acknowledge the fact that the victim suffered from an illness and to assist the survivors through an acknowledgment of the suicide. At the same time, they can be spared the additional pain of having their loved one denied normal funeral rituals.

The Rabbinic Tradition also separates the ritual needs of the mourners from the rites due the deceased. This striking distinction is drawn in the Talmud in the rare occurrence of willful suicide. Rites such as rending clothing, eulogizing, and other services to the remains are not practiced. In contrast, rituals that are directed to the mourners — forming rows to escort the mourners from the grave, the traditional benediction for mourners and other acts of consolation — are still practiced. The Talmud states that even in the case of willful suicide, "We occupy ourselves with anything that makes for respect of the living."[18]

Conclusion

Because God is the grantor of life, the taking of any life including one's own, except under very limited circumstances, is prohibited in Jewish Tradition. The accounts in the Hebrew Bible and statements in Rabbinic Tradition make clear that Jewish Law considers most suicides irrational acts committed by persons who are not to be held responsible for their actions. Even if, under very narrow conditions, the suicide is deemed culpable, the family is not denied those mourning rituals intended for the well-being of the living. In the modern world this means that in counseling and serving such families, the Jewish community can at once acknowledge the occurrence of a suicide, and at the same time not hold the deceased responsible for his or her own death. This permits full funeral rituals and an honorable burial.

Conversely, Jewish Tradition would be opposed to so-called "rational" suicide as the antithesis of Judaism's affirmation of life. Committed to the idea that this life is our most significant concern and that we ought not to pass into the next life until we are summoned by God, we are prohibited from knowingly hastening our own death. Therefore, within the Jewish understanding of suicide, it is precisely the "rational suicide" that is condemned and rejected.

Further, the limited but significant Biblical evidence shows the Hebrew Bible to be opposed to assisted suicide. The fact that the Rabbinic Tradition is silent indicates that the possibility of assisting a suicide was not contemplated in the classical literature's consideration of suicide. Prematurely ending life, even upon request is, within Jewish Tradition, nothing short of murder.

In conclusion, the thrust of the Hebrew Bible and Rabbinic Tradition's teaching in the field of suicide is, as in all things, animated by the biblical command to "choose life." Suicidal behavior is to be treated as a life-threatening illness with those around the patient responsible for saving his or her life. The suicide victim is almost never held to be sinful or guilty for having succumbed to the emotional or physical pain that leads to suicide. The survivors are, at all times, to be treated with the compassion shown any other mourners whose lives are shattered by a tragic and painful death.

Notes

1. The term "Hebrew Bible" refers to the books from Genesis through Chronicles or those books in the Jewish canon. The term is preferred over "Old Testament" by those faith traditions that do not accept the "New Testament" as authoritative scripture.
2. Rabbinic Tradition refers to and is here used as the equivalent of the post-biblical Jewish Law represented in the Mishnah, Gemara (together being the Talmud), Codes and other bodies of the Oral Law.
3. See Leviticus 22:33; Babylonian Talmud, Sanhedrin 74a.
4. Shulchan Aruch, Yoreh Deah 345:4.
5. Judges 9:50-57.
6. Judges Chapter 16.
7. Judges 16:30.
8. See and read together, I Samuel 31:1 through II Samuel 1:16.
9. II Samuel 17:23.
10. I Kings 16:8-20.
11. The verb also occurs in the reflexive form *mitabaid*.
12. Deuteronomy 26:5.
13. Babylonian Talmud, Semahot 2:1; Shulchan Aruch, Yoreh Deah 345:1; Mishneh Torah, Hilchot Evel 2:11.
14. Genesis Rabbah 34:19; Mishneh Torah, Rotzeah 2:3; other comments and exegesis on Genesis 9:5.
15. Babylonian Talmud, Semahot 2:2.
16. Mishneh Torah and Shulchan Aruch as cited above.
17. Shulcan Aruch, Yoreh Deah 345:3.
18. Babylonian Talmud, Semahot 2:1; also see Shulchan Aruch, Yoreh Deah 345:1,2.

Glossary

Midrash	Literally exposition, Rabbinic Interpretations of the Bible
Mishneh Torah	Important code of Jewish Law by Moses Maimonides (1135-1204)
Shulchan Aruch	Authoritative code of Jewish Law by Joseph Caro (1488-1575)
Talmud	Basic text of Jewish Law and Lore

Bibliography

Goldstein, Sidney, *Suicide in Rabbinic Literature*, Ktav, 1989.

Interpreter's Dictionary of the Bible, Abington, 1962/1981, see brief article at 4: 453.

Mishneh Torah of Maimonides, Hilchot Evel & Hilchot Rotzeah.

Principles of Jewish Law, Menachem Elon, ed., *Encyclopaedia Judaica*, 1975, page 477.

Shulchan Aruch, Yoreh Deah.

Tanakh, The Holy Scriptures, Jewish Publication Society translation of the Hebrew Bible, 1985.

Tractate Sanhedrin, Babylonian Talmud.

Tractate Semahot, Babylonian Talmud.

Universal Jewish Encyclopedia, Ktav, 1943/1969, 10: 93.

Chapter 2

A Catholic Perspective on Suicide

John A. Gallagher, Ph.D.

In the not too far distant past, Catholic pastoral practice toward suicidal persons and their families was consistent and clear. Suicide was viewed as a grave moral evil, a mortal sin, which separated the Catholic Christian from communion with God. The role of the pastor was to instruct the suicidal person regarding the moral and religious gravity of his/her contemplated act and to marshal whatever spiritual or psychological resources necessary in order to prevent suicide completion. Since Vatican II there has been considerable discussion among Catholic theologians which has prompted an alternative to the traditional Catholic pastoral approach to the issue of suicide. The task of this brief essay will be to track some of the more significant aspects of this theological evolution and to indicate their implications for Catholic pastoral care.

The traditional pastoral approach to suicide

Catholic pastoral care in the pre-Vatican II church can be characterized by two interrelated characteristics — it was both sacramental and moralistic. The ministry of the church was construed as being fulfilled through the administration of the seven sacraments. It was principally through those sacraments that Catholics experienced the saving and healing grace of Christ. Baptism and confirmation brought new Catholics into the community of grace and strengthened them in their relationship to God. Confession (Reconciliation) enabled sinful Catholics to re-establish their relationship to God. Extreme Unction (Anointing of the Sick) prepared the dying for union with God. The Eucharist, the frequent celebration of the Mass, nourished the lives of Catholic Christians and deepened their relationship to God. Marriage and Ordination, the two vocational sacraments, established Catholics into particular ways of life. Since Catholic pastoral care was so pervasively sacramental, it was also pervasively priestly. Only an ordained priest authorized by the local bishop could properly administer the sacraments. Indeed there were other ministries within the church such as religious education and care of the sick and orphaned. But whether these activities were carried on by priests, non-ordained religious, or the laity, they were deemed good works, inspired by, but distinct from the pastoral care of the church — the administration of the sacraments.

Pre-Vatican II Catholic pastoral care was moralistic because the theology which supported this ministry was moral theology rather than the theology of the sacraments themselves. As seminarians prepared for their roles as administrators of the sacraments, priests were required to learn the legal (Canon law) requirements for the proper administration of each sacrament. In order to hear properly the confessions of penitents, the priest was required to be able to assess the nature of sins that might be confessed (whether they were mortal or venial, which commandment or virtue a sin violated, whether the person was culpable for the sin) as well as the number of times individual sins might have occurred. Moral theology, the seminary course which enabled priests to identify the nature and number of sins and introduced them to the Canon law of the sacraments, served as the primary vehicle of pastoral education for generations of priests. Effective pastoral care was measured in relation to the standards established in moral theology.

The textbooks in moral theology framed the approach of pre-Vatican II pastoral care toward suicide. Moral theology argued for the inherent moral evil in suicidal acts on both theological and moral grounds. Theologically, suicide involved moral evil because it was viewed as an act of dominion over a good (life) which was properly a possession of God, not a possession of men or women (Noldin, 1908). John McHugh and Charles Callan (1930) stressed essentially the same point in asserting that persons did not have authority over their own lives or those of others. Theologically the moral evil associated with suicide consisted in the hubris of human beings exercising control over what belonged to God. Current discussions of the sanctity and stewardship of life are the contemporary refinements of these theological considerations.

Moral theology also marshaled natural law arguments against suicide. According to the English Jesuit Henry Davis (1935), suicide constituted "the greatest perversion of a rational nature." Similarly, McHugh and Callan (1930) described suicide as an act "against the deepest natural inclination for self-preservation and against self-love." The natural law arguments construed the drive for self preservation as ordering human beings to a fundamental good: life. An act which directly destroyed that good was assessed as a mortal sin. Indeed, natural law arguments interpreted suicide not only as a moral evil against an inclination toward life which God the Creator had implanted into human nature, but also as a moral evil which violated the additional divinely given inclination to live together in society.

The theological and moral (natural law) elucidations of the evils associated with suicide pertained to what was called objective morality (Gallagher, 1990). The purpose of objective morality was to elucidate God's will and the manner in which He ordered human affairs. Divine and natural laws mediated God's will to human beings — they constituted an objective moral ordering of the human universe. This was clearly a theocentric ethic in which God's will, not human will, was the moral measure of human acts.

Moral theology, however, also addressed the subjective aspect of morality. The pole of human morality dealt with the capacity of the human intellect to know God's will and the ability of human will to conform to it. Ignorance of moral law removed or diminished one's responsibility for objectively sinful acts. Such ignorance could either be vincible, in which case one should have known the law, or invincible, whereby one could not be reasonably expected to know a particular moral law. For example, the common soldier could not be expected to be able to determine the moral rightness or wrongness of a given war, but the head of state and generals could be expected to do so. In an immoral war, the moral responsibility of the infantry soldier was viewed as significantly less than that of higher authorities. Fear, coercion, or force could mitigate the will's responsibility for embracing specific evil acts. The moral culpability for some acts was reduced by threats, dangers, and coercion. Note, however, that although defects of knowledge and freedom could alter the responsibility of a person for an evil act, the act itself retained its full moral heinousness.

Objectively considered, moral theology deemed suicide a mortal sin. This was the starting point for pre-Vatican II pastoral care of suicidal parishioners and their families. However, the subjective aspect of morality outlined characteristics of the suicidal person that might diminish his/her responsibility for such an act. The general presumption of Catholic priests with regard to *post factum* suicides was that the person had been insane and thus not culpable for the moral consequences of the act. Despite the objective moral evil of suicide, Bernard Häring counseled his readers that one ought not judge the subjective guilt of anyone who takes his/her own life. We must, according to Häring (1966), presume the presence of "an acute mental disturbance."

In light of this theology, the pastoral task of a priest counseling a suicidal person was twofold. First the priest had the obligation to instruct the person concerning the moral gravity of his/her contemplated action — i.e., what the person was considering was a mortal sin, an objectively grave matter, an act capable of eternally separating the person from God. Second, the priest needed to counsel and assist the suicidal person to diminish that impact of those forces upon him/her that might compel consent to such a grievous act. The priest might offer personal and spiritual assistance to the suicidal parishioner. He might direct him/her to a psychiatrist or psychologist. Whatever human, medical, or spiritual forces the priest could marshal were to be employed to assist the person in the prevention of suicide.

These two tasks of pre-Vatican II Catholic pastoral care indicate the primary and underlying conception of pastoral care within this theology. The task of pastoral care was to facilitate, through the divine and natural laws, the individual Christian's effort to conform his/her will to that of God. The pastor was to insure that persons whom he was advising were, first, aware of the requirements of the law, and second, that obstacles to willingly conforming to the law were removed. In other words, the pastor was to tell the people that what they should do, and how they should live and mold the moral dimensions of their lives, are to be determined by the will of God. The person was not to be creative in this aspect of life. Indeed there were aspects of Christian life in which freedom to choose between two or more goods encouraged self-determination, i.e., choice of a state of life, career choices, or good works which exceeded the demands of morality. The aim of pastoral care in all cases involving moral issues such as suicide, however, was to facilitate the process by which a person could conform his/her will to that of God.

Contemporary Catholic pastoral care and suicidal persons

Vatican II unleashed forces within Roman Catholicism that would cultivate a reconsideration of ministry and pastoral care. The Word of God was returned to a position of preeminence within the Catholic ministry. "In the sacred books," *Dei Verbum* asserted, "the Father who is in Heaven meets His children with great love and speaks with them; and the force and power in the word of God is so great that it remains the support and energy of the Church, the strength of faith for her sons" (Abbott, 1966). Indeed *Dei Verbum* reaffirmed the ministry of the word as a source of nourishment which yields the fruit of holiness (Abbott, 1966). The ministry of the word emerged from Vatican II as a partner to sacramental ministry.

The introduction of a non-sacramental ministry within Catholicism made possible the emergence of non-ordained ministers. Religious men and women, as well as members of the laity, began to function in ministerial roles which previously would have been filled by priests. Non-ordained Catholic ministers function as pastoral counselors and hospital chaplains. The ministry of the word enabled groups of religious men and women to align their health care and educational ministries within the total mission of the Church. The preparation of men and women for this ministry is not exclusively the seminary; Catholic colleges and universities have undertaken a large portion of this task. The education of non-ordained ministers is not just theological. It is likely to include literary, sociological, and psychological training. Although ecclesiastical endorsement is part of the process, a substantial element in the credentialling of these ministers is through professional organizations. Ministry within the aegis of Roman Catholicism is no longer an exclusively priestly and sacramental ministry.

The moral dimensions of pastoral care are construed differently by those engaged in the ministry of the word and those involved in the sacramental ministry. The latter remain a key element in the spectrum of Catholic pastoral care. The Vatican's 1980 Declaration on Euthanasia essentially repeats the manualists' arguments against suicide. The former, however, simply do not have the need to determine the nature and number of specific sins. Their ministry does not extend to the sacrament of Reconciliation. Although the ministry of the word seeks to assist Christians in the avoidance of sin, it focuses on positive moral duties — i.e., what ought to be done. It is hardly surprising that a different theological paradigm underlies this ministry. Indeed there may well be a number of such paradigms currently at work in contemporary Catholic pastoral care, for instance Regis Duffy's provocative suggestion of the catechumenate model of pastoral care (1983). Latin American liberation theology offers yet another paradigm, but the more prevalent among American Catholics views Christian practice as directed by one's response to God's initiative.

This response paradigm was introduced into American Catholic thought through Bernard Häring's *The Law of Christ* (1966) and the many essays of Charles Curran (1970, 1972, 1977) which refined and gave nuance to the model. Although this model respects the value of moral rules, it also looks to the consequences of actions. It views the moral agent as existing within a communitarian social environment. This paradigm fundamentally differs from the pre-Vatican II pastoral care in its understanding of the Christian before God.

The traditional paradigm construed the Christian as passive — as conforming his or her will to the divinely established moral order. The response paradigm interprets the Christian as active before God. The Christian responds to God's initiatives in the forces of life, including cultural and religious forces. Theological traditions, narratives or stories, a theological stance, and membership within a believing community enable the Christian to respond to the events and moral quandaries of life. In doing so, the Christian creates a living, fitting response to the array of forces that shape his/her moral environment.

This paradigm proposes a significantly different task for pastoral care. The pastor's task in this case is not simply the clarification of a pre-given moral order and the provision of resources essential for a person to conform his/her will to that order. The task of pastoral care engendered by the response model suggests a discernment of duties and responsibilities. The pastor serves as a resource to assist the Christian in reading the divine initiative and crafting a response which fits the initiative — a response which reflects the religious, social and personal identity of the Christian and thus an embodiment of his/her love of God and neighbor.

The care extended to a suicidal person and his/her family from such a pastor might well differ from that offered by the traditional model. Certainly, this model retains the notion of life as a sacred gift which is to be respected. However, it also might offer a distinct perspective on some of the religiously and morally complex events that can occur in people's lives. Pastoral care facilitated by the response paradigm would direct the suicidal person's attention to the divine initiative in life and would strive to facilitate responses from him/her that might alter the social, familial, or personal elements of the world that make life appear to be so burdensome. The ultimate goal of such a process would be for the suicidal person to identify a response fitting to a context composed of the communitarian reality of existence as well as the religious, philosophical, and socio-cultural sources of meaning. In such a context, how ought the suicidal person and his/her family respond to a divine initiative? Discernment of the divine would strive to lead the suicidal person and his/her family toward the discovery of meaning and value within the apparently irrational forces of life.

In life and in death the Christian needs to be aware that he/she exists in a universe governed by providence, not fate. In life and in death the Christian must strive to avoid despair and to discover the sustaining force of hope, the virtue which opens Christians, "as though through a glass darkly," to the mystery of divine providence.

References

Abbott WM (editor): "Dei Verbum" in *The Document of Vatican II*. New York, Guild Press, 1966, pages 125-127.

Curran C: *Catholic Moral Theology in Dialogue*. Notre Dame, Fides Publishers, Inc., 1972, page 32.

Curran C: *Contemporary Problems in Moral Theology*. Notre Dame, Fides Publishers Inc., 1970, pages 235-238.

Curran C: *Themes In Fundamental Moral Theology*. Notre Dame, University of Notre Dame Press, 1977, pages 136-139.

Davis H: *Moral and Pastoral Theology*, II Precepts. London, Sheed and Ward, 1935, page 115.

Duffy R: *A Roman Catholic Theology of Pastoral Care*. Philadelphia, Fortress Press, 1983.

Gallagher J: *Time Past, Time Future*. New York, Paulist Press, 1990, pages 75-97 provides a more extensive discussion of the objective and subjective aspects of pre-Vatican II moral theology.

Häring B: *The Law of Christ* in 3 volumes. Translated by Kaiser EG. Westminister, Newman Press, 1966.

Häring B: *The Law of Christ*, Vol. III Special Moral Theology. Translated by Kaiser EG. Westminister, The Newman Press, 1966, page 220.

McHugh J, Callan C: *Moral Theology*. New York, John F. Wagner Inc., 1930, page 1854.

Noldin H: *Summa Theologiae Moralis*, II De Praeceaptis. Innsbruck, Felix Rauch, 1908, page 343.

"Vatican Declaration of Euthanasia." *Origins* 9: 154-157, 1980.

Chapter 3

A Protestant Perspective on Suicide

Herbert Anderson, Ph.D.

It is appropriate that the Protestant perspective on suicide be presented last in this series of three because it has been shaped by its origins in Judaism and Roman Catholicism. As a matter of fact, Protestantism does not add anything very new to a theological perspective on suicide. Therefore what I want to propose are a set of five theological propositions about life, death, and faith that have been or still are held by Protestants and that set the agenda for a theological discussion regarding suicide.

(1) Life is a gift from God

We may not all believe that God literally breathes life into each individual person, but most would agree that in general life begins with God. If it is true that life is God's gift, then, it has been said, it is not our decision to take life back. My father used to announce whenever someone died in the parish, "It has pleased the Lord in his infinite wisdom to call from our midst John Johnson at (such and such an age). The Lord gives and the Lord takes, praised be the name of the Lord." Most will agree with the first half of the statement — that we have life as a sacred trust, a gift from God.

We would not all agree, however, that God takes life — especially the life of a young parent, a small child, or someone we love. Instead, we are inclined to give death independent power to act. So we say death took or death came, as if death were an autonomous agent. I suspect that part of the reason is to make death something disconnected from life — or at least human life in general and "my" life in particular. If God does not take life and if death is not an independent agent, can we say death is a human act? When we acknowledge that "I will die" or "George died," do we intend to say something different than that God takes life or that death comes? We may die because of forces acting on us over which we have little or no control. And yet we believe that dying is something human beings do. "I am dying," we will say. If that is so, then suicide introduces a third question: can I ever decide when my life should be over and take action that causes my death?

For Dietrich Bonhoeffer, the answer to that question is a resounding NO! Bonhoeffer, a Lutheran pastor who was a leader of the resistance movement against Hitler, is quite clear about suicide. "God has reserved to himself the right to determine the end of life, because God alone knows the goal to which it is God's will to lead it... Even if a person's earthly life has become a torment, he or she must commit it intact to God's hand, from which it came" (Bonhoeffer, 1955). Because life is a gift from God we are not free to reject it. From this principle, our responsibility is to be faithful stewards of life that comes to us as a gift from God. Acting to cause death, from this point of view, is a violation of God's trust.

(2) God will not give us any more suffering than we can endure

That brings us to the second general theological principle that informs Protestant consideration of suicide. *God will not give us any more suffering than we can endure.* From that perspective, suicide may be understood as an act of unfaith because it presumes to set limits on how much suffering we think we can endure. Suicide is a denial of the promise that God's grace will be enough for the troubles of today. This perspective is also grounded in the conviction that suffering that is unbearable may still be meaningful.

Although it is common to say that suffering can teach us or suffering can become the occasion for personal growth, Protestants generally do not hold the belief that suffering is redemptive. Nor would we hold the belief that all suffering has meaning, even though enduring suffering may be an expression of Christian vocation. We face another complex pastoral question that has theological implications: how do we determine that the suffering we are experiencing has no meaning or divine purpose? And how do we decide if or when the combination of our resources and the promised resources of God together are not enough to endure the pain we feel? The sad truth is that most of us could endure more pain than we think. But because suffering is always in the eyes of the beholder, some decide prematurely and absolutely how much pain they can tolerate. In my judgment, one of the deeper societal problems undergirding the increase in suicide is the growing intolerance of pain. We expect a painless existence, or a "quick fix" that will make the pain go away. From the perspective of faith, suicide is not the solution to suffering but the promised presence of God is.

(3) We promote life although we never possess it

The phrase "Promote Life" that was a slogan for the conference that gave birth to this book reflects a major religious conviction regarding life: more life is better life. Most of the time. But not always. Sometimes when the quality of human life is severely limited or hardly present, it becomes understandable if someone decides that more life in a quantitative sense is intolerable. And if suicide is an understandable choice, is it ever a theologically acceptable option? If we cannot say with certainty that more life is always better life, is it ever possible to decide in advance in favor of human action that shortens life?

In every religious tradition and for every religious practitioner, our first, second, and third impulse is to promote life — not in a minimalist way but in an extravagant way. Jesus came, we are told, so that people might have abundant life — full life — life sustained by the extravagant promises of God. Such extravagant living is seldom easy, never perfect, always risky, and always costly. We are called to give our life away. It is not ours to possess. The relationship between suicide and self-sacrifice is far more complex than would appear on the surface. To some people, from some perspectives, that way of living may look a little like Shneidman's (1985) category of sub-intentioned death. A life of service may seem to be self-destructive. To say that the ones who "lose their lives will find life" introduces a fundamental paradox into our consideration of life and death. This third theological proposition requires a delicate balance of contrary impulses: *we promote life although we never possess it.*

(4) None of us can see all there is to see and endure

No one can look at the sun and live, Rilke has reminded us. Or to put it another way, it is only God who neither slumbers nor sleeps. That is the fourth theme that is both psychologically necessary and theologically true. All of us at one time or another in our life would like to assume the fetal position, turn the electric blanket up to nine, play a tape of ocean waves, and hope that sooner or later *it* will all go away. It is not far from that posture to conclude that since *it* will not go away — whatever *it* is — then I must go away. *The recognition that none of us can see all there is to see and endure is one of the reasons why we are cautious in our judgments of suicidal persons.*

The novel *Jude the Obscure*, written by Thomas Hardy at the turn of the century, continues to haunt me — particularly when I think of the suicide of children. In this novel, Jude and his family fall on hard times. His wife, Sue, is pregnant and they are homeless. She and her firstborn, young Jude, and two younger children wander through rainy streets in search of lodging. Young Jude, who is a very sensitive and reflective child, despairs that he has been born. During the night, young Jude kills his younger siblings and then hangs himself. In an effect to comfort his wife, the elder Jude says, "it was his nature to do it. The doctors say there are such boys springing up amongst us — boys of a sort unknown in the last generation — the outcome of new views of life. They seem to see all its terrors before they are old enough to have staying power to resist them. The doctors say it is the beginning of the coming universal wish not to live" (p. 331). Hardy wrote that in 1895, at a time when the changes occurring were pale in comparison to changes in our present time.

What is relevant about the quote for our time is that there are many people, some of them children, who see all of the terrors of life before they have the emotional capacity to tolerate what they see and know. The poet Edwin Brock has captured this human plight with these lines: "You will not see the world at first, you will touch the flesh and you will cry. Years later you will cry because you see too much and touch too little."

For some people, there are really only two options: suicide or apathy. By apathy I mean the social condition in which people are dominated by the goal of avoiding suffering. Suicide and apathy are both terrible moral choices. One is psychic death and the other is physical death. Unless we learn how to suffer and live with those who suffer, these will become more and more frequent options. I believe it is essential that we find ways of entering into our despair, if only for a brief moment, in order to suffer and live. Perhaps a companion volume should be devoted to the topic of enduring pain.

(5) Provide a full ministry of care to those who survive suicide

One last principle: *even if there is still general disapproval of suicide on theological grounds, that should not prevent us from providing full ministry of care to those who survive.* We would all agree to this as a general principle even though it is sometimes difficult to implement in the particular. People are more important than the sanctity of rituals or the purity of dogma. The tragic truth is that the survivors are the ones who are often punished for a death by suicide. For example, in England, it was not possible until 1882 for someone who died by suicide to have a normal burial. There is a statement in a Presbyterian document on "the nature and value of human life" that reflects this general shift toward a more compassionate point of view: "Whatever our judgment about the morality of actions in this sphere — we should never call into question the abounding love of God for those pointed to such anguished acts of self-destruction."

Our pastoral response to those who are suicidal is to promote life carefully and realistically — without at the same time denying the terror or despair that precipitated the suicidal thoughts in the first instance. We may be their hope until they get the help they need. Our pastoral response to those who are suicide survivors is to sustain them in their particular grief. Our sustaining ministry will in fact promote grief for the sake of the living. In order not to complicate their grief any further, *all* normal religious resources should be available to suicide survivors. Even if we do not approve of suicide theologically, we need to care for the survivors fully.

The effectiveness of our pastoral ministry with those who contemplate suicide hinges in part on our ability to be empathic. Whether or not we approve of suicide from a theological perspective is not the central issue in the final analysis: the central issue is our willingness to understand the pain and suffering that would prompt someone to contemplate suicide. There is a risk to empathy. If we can understand why someone might wish to die, then it might be more difficult to condemn every suicide as an act of unfaith. It is a risk worth taking, however, because people are more important than proper theology.

References

Bonhoeffer D: *Ethics*. New York, MacMillan, 1955, pages 124-125.
Hardy T: *Jude The Obscure*. New York, New American Library, 1961 (1980), page 331.
Shneidman E: *Definitions of Suicide*. New York, John Wiley and Sons, 1985, pages 20-22.

III. *Fundamental Knowledge and Skills for Clergy*

Introduction

Each of the next five chapters is focused on a body of fundamental knowledge, skills, and attitudes that every pastor ought to have in his/her quiver. Is it possible to recognize suicide risk, and where does one begin? Chapter 4 highlights information, skills, and attitudes that provide the pastor with some basis for recognizing subtle, unfolding suicidal crises. The chapter is organized around a case illustration, permitting the reader to participate in the assessment, reach his/her own conclusions, and compare conclusions with those of the "experts."

After one has recognized suicide risk, what should one do next? Some pastors possess the training, background, and experience to undertake psychotherapy with persons recognized to be suicidal, and Chapter 5 is intended for them. Chapter 5 features a case illustration of a suicidal adolescent boy. The vignette is accompanied by three brief explications of different psychotherapeutic approaches by three psychotherapists representing "client-centered," "cognitive," and "integrative-eclectic" schools of psychotherapy.

Some pastors will choose to refer persons who may be suicidal to a qualified mental health professional. How can the pastor determine which local mental health professionals are qualified to assess and manage suicide risk? How should the referral be implemented? Can referrals be engineered so that the pastor continues to participate as a member of the treatment team? These issues are discussed at length in Chapter 6.

The suicidal person is not our only source of concern. Chapter 7 addresses the plight of family members of persons who experience suicidal impulses, who make suicide attempts, or who die by suicide. How can the cleric minister effectively to those who live in dread of a family member's death by suicide?

Counseling frequently gives rise to sticky questions about how to manage information that was shared with the pastor in confidence. One such problem is posed obliquely by the case illustration in Chapter 4. In Chapter 8, Dr. Burton discusses whether a clergyperson has a "duty to warn others" about a congregant's expressed intent to commit suicide, a duty that supersedes the usual parameters of confidentiality.

Chapter 4

Recognizing Suicidal Risk

Rev. Dan G. Stauffacher, D. Min.
and David C. Clark, Ph.D.

It is not always easy, and sometimes it is *difficult*, to recognize
when another person shows the signs and features that define
serious risk for suicidal behavior. The problem is compounded
when the person we want to help is slow to recognize his/her
own psychological symptoms, resists talking about his/her feelings and thoughts, insists the chief problem is an *external* one, or
intentionally blocks well-meaning efforts to be helpful. The case
of Sam, which follows, is instructive in these regards, and so we
will discuss Sam in some detail after outlining the facts of the
case. The circumstances have been altered to protect Sam's identity and that of his family. We are indebted to Howard Sudak, M.D.
for his help in developing this case illustration for teaching purposes.

I. The case of Sam

Sam, a 42-year-old married white male insurance agent and
church deacon, made an appointment with his minister because
of increasing guilt about an extramarital affair that has been going
on for six years. He has been married for 18 years and has two
children, a boy 16 and a girl 13. Although he described the marriage as generally a good one, Sam began to feel the "excitement
had gone out of his life" soon after their second child was born.
Later that year his secretary became widowed, and Sam began to

take a more personal interest in her, which progressed over the years from paternal to affectionate, culminating in a sexual relationship throughout the last six years. Sam has never seen a therapist or counselor before, and did not feel particularly guilty until three or four weeks before he made the appointment.

In his second meeting with Rev. Smith, Sam continues to talk about how guilty he feels. He feels his behavior was not just unfair to his wife, but morally sinful as well. He is convinced that God will punish him for his transgressions, and can think of practically nothing else. He reports sitting for hours at work ruminating about what a bad person he is. He has not been able to concentrate on his work for several weeks, and several co-workers have commented on lapses in the quality of his work. He decided to stop seeing the secretary, but that did not diminish his guilt.

In the next two meetings with Rev. Smith, it is obvious that Sam is losing weight. He describes waking unusually early (e.g., 4:00 a.m.) without being able to fall back asleep, and intermittent spells of weeping at work and at home. He has missed several successive weekly golf outings with his friends, which is unusual for him. He is less interested in spending time with his children. He has a gun at home, but assures Rev. Smith that he would never use the gun to kill himself, because he doesn't want to offend God any more than he already has.

Sam's wife grows increasingly concerned about his state as he becomes more quiet and sullen at home. She is puzzled and upset by his behavior. She has no knowledge of the affair. She repeatedly presses him to see a doctor. Sam dismisses the idea as "a waste of time and money." He says he feels comfortable talking with the minister, and trusts him to respect the confidentiality of their conversations. Rev. Smith decides to increase the frequency of their meetings from once to twice per week. Sam continues to keep all his appointments, but grows increasingly nervous and fidgety. Two months after he first consulted Rev. Smith, Sam calls to say he can not continue to come in and talk, and refuses to give any explanation.

II. Case analysis — Rev. Stauffacher

The clergy as part of a larger treatment team

The case of Sam is not uncommon to any of us in the course of our pastoral work. In all probability, we each may know a "Sam." In the next section, Dr. Clark will review this case through the eyes of a trained mental health professional. His comments will be helpful to us and will stretch us to see more than an untrained eye might see. We, however, are *not* trained clinicians. We are clergy doing the day-to-day work of pastoral care. This work is not meant to duplicate or replace good clinical care where necessary. It simply is intended to augment that care.

In simple terms, we clergy need to see our role as being part of a larger treatment team that is concerned with the care of a person in Body, Mind and Spirit. As a vital part of that team, it is appropriate to see what we do as *different* from the work of physicians, therapists and social workers. We represent the sacred within the secular and bring with us both Testament and Sacrament with Covenant.

As with any of the work in our profession, we face equal potentials of great joy and danger when dealing with suicide. Here the joys are self-evident. We have a friend and parishioner who is able to regain health and face the rest of his life with renewed hope. However, there are at least four dangers. First, no matter how hard we work and no matter how skilled we are, the possibility always exists that someone may complete a suicide. This is a tragedy of immense proportion for the clergyperson involved, the family, and those who know the deceased. Thankfully, this is a rare phenomenon. If it does happen, the pastor should take the time to do his/her own grief work and avail him/herself of good pastoral and professional care. While he/she is at it, the pastor should do the same for the grieving community that has called him/her into their midst.

The second danger is that we face the possibility of forsaking our theological and historical heritage and becoming essentially secular therapists in the pastoral office. Sometimes this step is taken with appropriate training and sometimes not. Either way we must guard against the temptation to forget our primary calling. We are pastors, clergy of many faiths. This is a unique and special role in the community — most especially in dealing with suicide.

Among the general practitioners of the land, we still know what the living rooms and workplaces of our communities look like. The open invitation to visit people where they live and where they work becomes a valuable tool in determining risk relative to signs of depression or suicide. There is no foolproof way to predict whether a person will or will not attempt or complete suicide, but seeing them in various parts of their daily life certainly can help us to understand more of what is going on for them. Visiting parishioners is a pastoral tool and skill. Use it, and let it be guided by the pastor's faith and sacred calling. It is not the kind of visit a social worker or psychologist would make, but the kind made by a pastor giving "care."

Third on the list of dangers is the other extreme from being secular therapists in the pastoral office, namely, *forsaking* good psychological knowledge to rely solely on skills not fully suited to the problem at hand. Balance and proportion are necessary in all walks of life. Suicidal risk is no exception. We as clergy *need* to have some good counseling skills. The operating words here are "clergy" (with all that this means in each of our faith traditions) and "some." We are not expected to be all things to all people, but we do need to act with competence and professionalism. The use of monosyllabic pop-psyche clichés and assumptions that what we have to offer is all that is needed are incompetent, dangerous, and potentially litigious responses. Assessing and responding to suicide risk is best done as a part of a larger team. We are pastors with good faith and theological skills. We are able to call on the folk about whom we are concerned. We need to have some good counseling skills so that we can know when we are doing what is appropriate and when to refer people for more professional help.

Finally, the fourth danger, the issue of denial, must be faced. It can exist in ourselves and in our communities and manifests itself as variations on the theme of not wanting to see what is really there because:

(1) We do not want to get involved;

(2) It would be too embarrassing to a church member and includes consequences for us as clergy both financially and politically within our congregations;

(3) We see the behavior as simply some sort of temporary aberration, i.e., "just a phase they are going through;" and

(4) We do not believe what we see and doubt what we hear when someone tells us how hopeless they feel and that they want to "just go away forever."

Once we have moved past or through these dangers, our next task is to develop our skills as observers while holding fast to our faith, so that we can ask the tough questions if and when necessary. To be alert to persons who may be laboring under the influence of a depressive illness, we need to look for symptoms and behaviors that either: (a) represent a significant change for the person when compared to themselves over a period of time: or (b) involve alcohol abuse or other drug abuse. The behavior changes might be one or several of the following:

(1) **sleep** — more or less than usual, mid-sleep awaking without being able to go back to sleep, fitful non-restful sleep

(2) **weight** — significant change up or down without logical explanation (such as a medically supervised diet)

(3) **social activities** — much more/less than usual. In church this might be seen as someone who never volunteered for anything and now is volunteering for all sorts of tasks, or the opposite, the number one volunteer who begins to withdraw from everything

(4) **personal hygiene /self-care** — deteriorating

(5) **energy level** — way up or way down for more than a couple of weeks

(6) **irritable** — more than usual

(7) **sexual energy** — more or less than usual

(8) **sadness** — general mood change

(9) **hopelessness** — little hope for the future

(10) **suicide ideation** — talking about it, thinking about it

(11) **prior suicide attempt(s)**

Through pastoral eyes

With all this in mind, now let us look at the case of Sam through pastoral eyes. In the first visit between Sam and his minister three things became obvious: Sam's self-acknowledged guilt, Sam's denial, and the doubtful presence of a base of support in the family.

Sam's guilt is real and stems from a decision he has made to engage in a particular behavior. At this point, this alone is not a basis for suicidal alarm, but does make a case for pastoral care. His denial is a little more problematic. It is hard to understand the phrases "generally good marriage" and "extramarital affair" in the same paragraph. Again, these observations are not a basis for a suicidal alarm, but something that raises serious unanswered questions.

In the presence of the first two observations, one can presume a diminished quantity of support available to Sam. Affairs are generally structured to include their own form of denial, lying, avoidance, and self-serving narcissism.

It is interesting to note that the affair went on for six years before any guilt began to emerge. This still does not indicate any observable suicide risk, although it is an indication for competent counseling — both individual and marriage.

In the second session with his minister, Sam begins to identify how his current set of problems are beginning to disrupt his daily life schedule and structure. He reports concern about God punishing him for his transgressions; he can think of practically nothing else. "He reports sitting for hours at work ruminating about what a bad person he is." His concentration at work has been impaired for weeks, there are difficulties with co-workers, and he begins to withdraw from his relationships with the secretary and with family members. He reports having a gun at home but says he would never use it to kill himself because that would constitute another sin and he does not want to offend God any more than he already has.

Following these revelations, there is a litany of physical complaints. At this point, competent pastoral care would be guided not to try to deal with all these issues in a vacuum, but rather to suggest to Sam that he seek a medical consultation with either a family physician or a professional therapist. Suicide concern is now evident. This concern is intensified when Sam's wife suggests he see a doctor and Sam refuses. His refusal has the capacity to further erode the support available at home as well as increase stress, both of which can exacerbate the problems with which Sam is dealing.

These problems continue to worsen over a period of two months, and then the counseling sessions end abruptly with no explanation. There is serious and significant cause for concern at this point. It is time for a home visit to discuss with Sam the seriousness of what has been going on with him and invite his permission to include his wife in the conversation. There is no indication that Sam will agree to this, but it is worth a try.

Pastoral care-giving

Pope Gregory reminds us that each case of pastoral care-giving requires variable responses. This is especially true in recognizing and responding to suicide risk. It is necessary to consider the whole person before individual suicide risk can be assessed. One must also be able to understand the interrelatedness of all the symptoms and issues in the person's life. As pastors we can do this by using a variety of skills and responses including:
(1) making home visits where appropriate;
(2) providing spiritual care;
(3) not being secular therapists in the pastoral office but learning how to make effective referrals;
(4) providing support to the Sams in our lives and their families;
(5) being an educator on the need for outside consultations and going with people if necessary;
(6) being a constant advocate for health — mental, physical, and spiritual;
(7) being tolerant of mood swings; and
(8) above all HAVING COURAGE to see the truth, speak the truth, and live the truth... in love and pastoral care.

III. Case analysis — Dr. Clark

The case of Sam begs us to consider two fundamental questions about how we respond to a fellow human being in distress: (a) Should we *always* take a distressed person's evaluation of his/her own crisis at face value? and (b) Should we *always* confine our interpretations of human distress to the spiritual or moral spheres? If one is prone to answer "yes" to either question, there is a great danger that the caregiver will inadvertently facilitate Sam's death by suicide.

Let us consider Rev. Smith's position in the case illustration posed. Rev. Smith has known Sam, his wife, and his children for many years. They are probably social friends, and have probably dined in one another's homes before. Since Sam is a church deacon, it is fair to suppose that Sam is a leader within the congregation, and that Rev. Smith feels a particularly acute obligation to help Sam when asked. It is also important to note that the Rev. Smith may be under some implicit pressure to respond to Sam in an *exemplary* way — after all, Sam is a deacon and friend whose satisfaction or dissatisfaction with the Rev. Smith's counseling may have repercussions throughout the rest of the congregation.

Sam asks Rev. Smith to address one sector of a crisis — Sam's guilt — and Sam does not want his wife, his physician, or anyone else to become involved. One way to understand the situation is to notice the degree to which Sam has tied Rev. Smith's hands: (a) Rev. Smith is asked to assuage guilt and help Sam feel that his sin has been forgiven, but the pastor is effectively forbidden to address any other aspects of Sam's problems; (b) Rev. Smith is forbidden to discuss the problems with Sam's wife or physician; and (c) Sam unilaterally decides when to stop meeting without any explanation.

Sam's narrow, rigid view of his difficulties is an important *symptom* of his illness. To accept Sam's definition of the problem and Sam's ground rules for counseling is to believe that he is psychologically well and has a complete, flexible view of his situation. But Sam is not well. He is laboring under the influence of major depressive illness — this is obvious in the case vignette — which has a destructive influence on his thinking, judgment, and behavior. Like so many people experiencing a depressive episode,

Sam has poor insight into his own situation. His judgment is severely compromised by his depressive illness, and his thinking is profoundly influenced by his despair, pessimism, and guilt. Indecision, confusion, fatigue, and a measurable drop in functional intelligence are common features of a depressive episode.

Rev. Smith knows from experience that Sam holds an intellectually demanding job, that church members entrust church business to Sam, and that Sam is a clever, thoughtful, and articulate fellow — when he is well. The pastor supposes that Sam *continues* to exercise sound judgment because he always has in the past — neither the pastor nor Sam recognize that Sam has developed an acute illness. Sam's lifetime history of positive mental health renders Rev. Smith slow to consider the possibility that Sam is experiencing a depressive illness. But depressive illness is typically a *transient* disorder that disrupts the lives of persons who were psychologically healthy beforehand. The list of talented public figures who have been afflicted with a severe mood disorder is long, and includes Ludwig van Beethoven, Abraham Lincoln, Winston Churchill, Patty Duke, William Styron, Dick Cavett, and Rod Steiger.

Why do I believe that Sam is severely depressed? First, it is important to notice that while Sam has had an ongoing sexual relationship with his secretary for the last six years, he "did not feel particularly guilty until three or four weeks before he made the appointment" to see Rev. Smith. Why would Sam fail to experience much in the way of guilt for five years and eleven months, then suddenly develop an unrelenting preoccupation with guilt that does not abate when he stopped seeing the secretary, or in response to spiritual counseling with his pastor? In this case, the guilt is a symptom of a severe depressive illness that began three or four weeks before Sam first came to Rev. Smith's office.

There are a number of other remarkable features consistent with a diagnosis of severe depressive illness. Sam feels that he deserves to be punished. His concentration at work is severely disrupted and co-workers recognize his work impairment. He is visibly losing weight, experiencing a sleep disturbance ("early morning awakening"), and has crying spells. He lost interest in favorite activities (e.g., golf outings, time with his children).

Depressive illness is almost always accompanied by thoughts about death and suicide. Persons with depressive illness are at increased risk for death by suicide simply by virtue of their diagnosis. In this case, three other features of Sam's condition point in the direction of serious suicide risk. First, he has a gun in the home and defends his wish to keep the gun there. Scientific studies clearly demonstrate that a window of opportunity in the form of gun availability at home raises the risk of death by suicide for depressed persons. Persons considering killing themselves with a gun often go to great lengths to convince caregivers that they would never use the gun for self-harm and that they are not at all suicidal — just prior to the time when they kill themselves with the same gun. It is important to remember that 60% of all persons (men and women alike) who die by suicide in the U.S. each year use a gun to effect death. Conversely, 47% of all firearm-related deaths in the U.S. each year are suicides.

The second clue to serious suicide risk comes in the form of Sam's insistence on confidentiality. His insistence bars Rev. Smith from collecting more information from Sam's wife and from sharing the pastor's concern about Sam's symptoms with her. The insistence bars Rev. Smith and Sam's wife from involving the family physician. In situations like this, the pastor's duty is to convene all available sources of information and help for a problem-solving conference. Has Sam's wife noticed other symptoms? Has she heard talk about death or suicide? Would a medical or psychiatric evaluation help clinch the diagnosis of a severe depressive illness? The important and sensitive question of maintaining confidentiality becomes less pertinent (legally and ethically) when a parishioner's life is at stake (see the chapter on "Confidentiality and Expressed Suicide Intent" later in this volume). One could honor Sam's insistence on confidentiality to be agreeable and responsive, to adhere rigidly to an arbitrary code of professional ethics, or to avoid recriminations and lawsuits — but what good is confidentiality if Sam is simply exploiting it as a veil to shield his suicidal intentions, or if Sam dies? In a situation like this, the alert pastor has sufficient evidence that the parishioner is severely depressed and poses genuine suicide risk. Thus I believe the pastor must over-ride confidentiality concerns to involve others and press for a psychiatric consultation.

The third clue to serious suicide risk is manifest in the subtle ways that Sam has tied Rev. Smith's hands. This pattern of hindrance comes to a head when Sam quits counseling without notice and refuses to provide any further explanations. Is Sam better? Is he angry with Rev. Smith? Has Sam decided to go ahead and kill himself? Among psychiatrists and psychologists who work with suicidal persons, "help negation" — that is, pushing away offered help — is widely recognized as a serious symptom of escalating suicide risk. If Rev. Smith has not broken confidence to involve Sam's wife and physician in his planning before this, he must act decisively when Sam quits counseling. The pastor has an obligation to warn Sam's wife and physician that Sam is laboring under the influence of severe depressive symptoms, that Sam has a gun at home, and that Sam has refused to talk about his problems any longer. There is no evidence that Sam's condition has improved or that his suicidal tendencies have lessened. The pastor, Sam's wife, and Sam's physician together may be able to formulate a plan of action — for example, prevailing on Sam to see the physician or a local psychiatrist.

It is a far better thing to act on the justified concern that Sam may try to kill himself than to "hope nothing bad happens" or to trust Sam will return for more counseling when he feels the need. The worst possible consequence of the pastoral initiatives recommended here is that Sam will become angry that his pastor overreacted and make public complaints against the pastor. For this reason the wavering or uncertain pastor might do well to consult with a trusted colleague or mental health professional for advice about whether action is justified — this tack allows a criticized pastor to justify his decisions based on professional consultation. The best possible consequence of pastoral initiative is that Sam's depressive illness will be assessed, diagnosed, and treated properly, resulting in three positive outcomes: (a) Sam will not remain at risk for suicide, but will live; (b) Sam will recover his ability to eat and sleep normally, his concentration, his interest in golf outings and his children, and his ability to perform at work; and (c) with recovery from the depressive episode, Sam may become interested in resuming counseling sessions with Rev. Smith, to discuss the spiritual implications of Sam's long-term affair. After the depressive illness has been treated and has remitted, Sam's sense of guilt and questions about whether he can be forgiven may be discussed in depth without interference from the cognitive confusion introduced by depressive illness.

Chapter 5

Responding to a Suicidal Crisis

Ira S. Halper, M.D.,
James D. McHolland, B.D., Ph.D.,
and George Polk, S.T.M., M.Div.

There are three facets to a suicide crisis: the spiritual, the medical, and the psychological. While we have a strong interest in the spiritual facet of suicidality, this facet is discussed explicitly in other chapters. Our focus will be the medical and psychological aspects of the suicide crisis. We will present several possible approaches to the treatment of a patient here named "Mark." The facts of his case have been altered somewhat to protect his identity and that of his family.

I. The case of Mark

Mark is a 15 year old Jewish male referred by a friend of his family. The initial phone call from the mother indicated that Mark was very depressed and suicidal, doing very poorly in school (D's and F's), and had no friends.

Mark is first seen for an interview with his parents, during which he has little to say. When seen alone, Mark confirms that he is depressed and wants to die. He admits that he has been depressed for a long time and dislikes his life. His love for music is all that has kept him alive. Mark plans to become a professional musician. He had been practicing his instrument several hours a day, but his parents took the instrument away as punishment for poor school performance. He feels he has no choice except to conform to his parents' expectations that he do well in school and prepare for a career in medicine. He hates and resents the absence of choice. Mark has a specific plan for taking his life — hanging. He feels he has nothing to live for other than music.

Further questions reveal that Mark's mother thinks poorly of herself and has sometimes been depressed and lacking in confidence. His older brother, however, has experienced much self-confidence and achievement by emulating their successful father, a physician.

II. The medical dimension

The medical dimension of suicide is often overlooked by non-physicians. Suicidality can appropriately be viewed as a symptom of a psychiatric, that is, a medical-psychiatric illness. In fact scientific studies consistently show that major psychiatric illnesses can be diagnosed in about 90% of completed suicides (Black and Winokur, 1990). About 50% of the suicides were clinically depressed at the time of the act. About 20% of the suicides occurred in patients suffering from chronic alcoholism or other substance abuse disorders. Approximately 10% of patients suffering from schizophrenia ultimately commit suicide.

Symptoms of depression include depressed mood; diminished interest or pleasure in activities; weight loss or weight gain when not dieting, or decrease or increase in appetite; insomnia or too much sleeping; physical agitation or physical slowing observable by others; fatigue or loss of energy; feelings of worthlessness, or excessive or inappropriate guilt; diminished ability to think or concentrate, or indecisiveness; and recurrent thoughts of suicide or a suicide attempt.

It is important to ask specific questions to assess the degree of suicide risk. Some professionals who are not accustomed to talking with suicidal persons are reluctant to ask these questions. There is a spectrum of suicidality, ranging from the fleeting thought of killing oneself in a mildly depressed individual to the well thought out plan of a person who is at high risk for suicide.

To intervene effectively in a suicidal crisis, it is necessary for the clergy as well as the mental health professional to have detailed information about the individual's thoughts and feelings regarding suicide.

In a tactful but direct way, subjects can be asked the following questions: Do you ever feel that life is not worth living? Do you ever feel like ending it all? How close have you come to killing yourself? What are your reasons for wanting to die? Can you think of reasons to live? What has stopped you from killing yourself? Have you told anyone about your wish to kill yourself? What do you imagine would happen if you succeeded in your plan to kill yourself? Have you tried to kill yourself in the past?

Details should be asked about contemplated suicide attempts. Does the person have a specific plan? Does the person have access to the means for carrying out a suicide (e.g., to guns or pills)? Details of past suicide attempts are equally important. "I cut my wrists" may mean anything from superficial scratches to serious wounds requiring sutures. "I took an overdose of pills" may mean anything from the ingestion of a few relatively harmless pills in the presence of another person to the ingestion of an entire bottle of pills with the potential to cause coma and death. We should comment on the so-called "suicide gesture." We are uncomfortable with this phrase. It is true that some suicide attempts are designed largely to manipulate the environment. Nevertheless, suicide attempts generally conceal a *variety* of motives, and so every attempt should be taken seriously.

Rapport can be enhanced and hope encouraged by statements such as, "You must be in a lot of pain to be thinking of killing yourself. Have you felt this bad before? Maybe this pain will go away as unhappiness has gone away in the past." The subject can be educated about the tragic consequences of suicide attempts gone awry, including brain damage and other major disabilities.

All three of the authors have a commitment to the psychotherapeutic treatment of suicidality. At the same time, the important role of medication and hospitalization in the treatment of severely depressed and suicidal persons should not be overlooked. The medical model cannot explain every case of depression, and medication cannot prevent every suicidal patient from killing himself.

Nevertheless, a number of antidepressant medications are available which produce good results in some suicidal depressions. Some individuals are suicidal because of a combination of a biological depression and psychosocial problems. A combination of antidepressant medication and psychotherapy can be effective in these cases. Other medications can be used to reduce the severe anxiety which appears to be a risk factor for suicide in depressed individuals.

Today, most depressed patients can be treated successfully in an outpatient setting. However, the hospital remains a protective environment which can be lifesaving for patients who cannot control their self-destructive wishes. Electroconvulsive therapy (i.e., "shock therapy") may be indicated for a small number of carefully selected patients whose illnesses do not respond even to aggressive treatment with antidepressant medication and psychotherapy. The prognosis in major depressive disorders is excellent today. Eighty to 90% of patients can be treated successfully with modern techniques of pharmacological treatment and psychotherapy.

We will now discuss three psychological approaches to the evaluation and treatment of Mark.

III. Client-centered therapy approach — Rev. Polk

The client-centered psychotherapy approach of Carl Rogers emphasizes empathic listening on the part of the counselor. From this perspective, the counselor would refrain from asking a barrage of questions. Rather, he/she would invite Mark to sit with him/her for a while. The counselor would share his deep concern about Mark's despair and would invite him to share his pain aloud.

Rogers (Rogers & Sanford, 1989; Duke & Nowicki, 1989) believed that people are born with the capacity to direct themselves in a healthy way toward a level of completeness called self-actualization. He believed that interference with this development in the form of conditional acceptance from the outside world can lead to psychopathology. It was Rogers' belief that individuals have the ability to change their behavior and will be empowered to change once they have the freedom to explore their internal and external life. The responsibility of the client-centered therapist is to produce an atmosphere in which the client can renew his/her striving for self-actualization as well as acceptance of self and begin once more to grow. Three attitudes on the part of the therapist are important for the success of the treatment: accurate and empathic understanding, caring, and genuineness.

In the vignette about Mark and his family, there seems to be a lot of history and judgment restricting Mark's choices. He experiences himself as being caught in a web of family expectations, yet he is struggling to be free. Mark seems to be using his school performance as a weapon against his parents. Mark and his parents cannot negotiate with one another. The role of the therapist is to stand in the gap and ease the tension so that Mark and his parents can come closer together.

Using this approach, the counselor would not question Mark's judgment but rather encourage him to share a wish for a life different than that of his father. Client-centered therapy is not challenging but accepting. The counselor would trust in the hidden power of Mark's silent and rational self, want Mark to know that he is there for him, and suggest meeting with Mark twice a week until he/she better understood Mark's life story. He/she would help Mark develop the power to live his own life and help his parents accept the necessity of allowing Mark to go his own way with respect to his career.

The client-centered therapist can and should share with Mark his/her concern about suicide. The counselor would say to Mark how much his death would grieve the counselor and hope that Mark would defer any self-destructive action for a while, so they could work together. In the interactions about suicide, the counselor would be speaking to that rational and healthy part of Mark's self which is motivated toward personal growth rather than death.

It is of particular interest that Carl Rogers attended the Union Theological Seminary to study for the ministry before receiving his Ph.D. in Psychology from Columbia University. Client-centered psychotherapy has been an appealing approach for nonmedical therapists. All therapists, including psychiatrists, can learn from Rogers about the importance of empathy, positive regard and genuineness, and about the presence of a healthy part of the psyche in even very sick patients. However, client-centered therapy does not appear to place enough importance on recent developments in the biology of psychological disorders. The client-centered approach may actually increase the risk of suicide in certain patients by relying too much on a self which has been temporarily disabled by illness and rendered unable to work with the therapist toward self-actualization.

IV. Cognitive therapy approach — Dr. Halper

A different psychotherapy approach combines the medical model and cognitive therapy model of Dr. Aaron Beck. Cognitive therapy is an active, structured and usually short-term form of psychotherapy. Its rationale is deceptively simple. The way an individual views the world has a major influence on his/her emotions and behavior. Cognitions (i.e., thoughts or mental pictures) are based on attitudes or assumptions developed from previous experiences. *Dysfunctional* cognitions often lead to unpleasant feelings and maladaptive behavior. For example, the depressed individual tends to have a negative view of his/her self, experiences, and future. A variety of cognitive and behavioral strategies are employed to help the individual recognize the connection between customary (i.e., *automatic*) thoughts, emotions, and behavior and help him/her to substitute reality-oriented interpretations for dysfunctional beliefs.

Cognitive therapy is a powerful treatment modality which was originally developed for use with depressed patients. The technique is well defined, and a treatment manual has been published (Beck and colleagues, 1979). Multiple studies have documented the effectiveness of cognitive therapy in the treatment of depression. The cognitive therapist would begin by taking a brief history from Mark and his parents together, including some questions about suicide. The therapist would then see Mark alone and ask more detailed questions about his wish to die. The therapist would note the family history of depression (the mother had been depressed) and consider the possibility of a biological depression based on genetic factors. The therapist would weigh the pros and cons of antidepressant medication and consider inpatient as well as outpatient care. Let us assume for purposes of discussion that Mark's depression was largely due to psychosocial factors and that medication was not indicated or should be deferred. Let us also assume that the risk of suicide was significant but not serious enough to warrant hospitalization.

Three basic features of cognitive therapy have recently been described by Drs. Weishaar and Beck (1990). *Collaborative empiricism* is the process by which the therapist and the patient work together to formulate the patient's beliefs as hypotheses to be tested rather than as "givens." Through Socratic dialogue, the therapist poses questions which reveal the patient's errors in logic. *Guided discovery* is the process by which the therapist uncovers the personal meaning of events with the patient. *Questioning* leads the patient to examine the source, the function, and the usefulness of his beliefs.

Cognitive therapy combines the warmth of a human relationship, the objectivity of science, and a hopeful attitude. This is a powerful combination which can be particularly effective in combating hopelessness. The success of cognitive therapy in reducing hopelessness is important because hopelessness is a major risk factor for suicide. Cognitive therapy is commonly used with outpatients and is effective in combination with medication for the treatment of hospitalized depressed individuals.

The following is a possible scenario for the use of cognitive therapy in the initial interview with Mark. The cognitive therapist would ask him what the evidence was for his belief that he had to conform to his parents' expectations and become a physician. In point of fact, parents cannot choose careers for their children, no matter how hard they might try. For this to occur, children must agree to have careers chosen for them. Assuming that Mark had a professional level of musical talent, and assuming he had the intellectual ability to get good grades in school, what would stop him from getting good enough grades to satisfy his parents and at the same time developing his knowledge and skills as a musician?

What would stop Mark from finishing school, getting a job, becoming financially independent and pursuing a musical career on his own? The therapist would help Mark to see the illogical nature of his belief that he has no choice of a career and challenge his underlying assumptions regarding his obligation to please his parents.

Because poor school performance apparently precipitated his parents' decision to take away his instrument and the resulting suicide crisis, the cognitive therapist would probably deal with this issue in the initial interview. The therapist would ask Mark what his ideas were about the reason for his poor school performance. Was he feeling hopelessness and unmotivated? Was he rebelling against his parents? Was school hard for him in an intellectual sense? Let us assume that Mark's poor performance was not due to lack of basic intellectual ability or to the intellectual deficits which can accompany severe depression. Let us also assume that the reasons for the poor school performance were hopelessness and rebellion. The therapist would challenge Mark's hopelessness and ask him how useful his chosen technique of rebellion was. The therapist would suggest that Mark consider a bargain with his parents. Mark would work hard in school to get better grades, and his parents would allow him to practice his instrument and pursue his musical studies. The choice of careers would be deferred to a later time.

If Mark could accept this bargain, the cognitive therapist would bring in his parents and tell them in Mark's presence that he/she sympathized with their frustration and understood their concern about Mark's future. The therapist would review with them the unfortunate consequences of their punishment, and ask them if they could join Mark and the therapist in a more positive short-term solution to the problem — namely the bargain described above. Assuming that both Mark and his parents could accept the bargain, Mark's level of depression and suicidality would be re-evaluated. Assuming he was less depressed and suicidal, the therapist would develop a treatment plan which would include individual cognitive therapy sessions for Mark and some conjoint visits with his parents. Cognitive therapy would be used in the conjoint sessions as well.

V. Integrative eclectic approach — Dr. McHolland

Mark and his parents did actually consult Dr. McHolland for treatment. Mark confirmed that he had been depressed for several years, did not like his life, and had a plan to kill himself by hanging. His love for music was the one thing he felt good about. The therapist asked whether Mark felt he had anything else going for him. Mark replied negatively, and so he was asked if he would still want to die if he could identify 50 things he liked about himself. When he answered, "No," the first intervention was underway.

Suicidal persons rarely like their own lives or feel self-confident. When a person feels suicidal self-hate, it is appropriate to intervene actively to provide a balance of realistic self-love. This intervention does not, by itself, eliminate the need for additional treatment to alleviate psychological pain associated with the identified problem areas.

The use of Dr. McHolland's method requires considerable effort to help the person identify and talk about specific strengths. The therapist had a clue from Mark that music was an area where he had real strengths. A depressed person tends to minimize strengths by talking about them in other ways, such as, "I like the fact that I like music." With Mark it was necessary to help him expand on his musical interests in the form of a series of strengths, talents, and passions. He was asked, "What instruments do you play? Do you like the way you play the guitar? How often do you practice? Is your practice enjoyable? Is that a strength? Do you ever compose music? Does it sound the way you want it to? *How* do you compose music? Is that a strength?" Mark and the therapist identified eight strengths in the area of music. Mark also felt his mother's love for him and the fact that he had one friend were strengths. While he was itemizing these strengths, the therapist was writing them on a pad of paper. After each strength was identified, the therapist slowly re-read the list to him. At the end, Mark was asked to read the list out loud, prefaced by, "I have these strengths in my life that I like." In some areas, he said he had no strengths. The therapist went on to another area, asking him about reading, nature, friends, religion, school subjects, teachers, sports, pets, his room, his hair, his mode of dress — anything that would enable him to confirm something of worth in his life.

At the end of the session Mark was asked whether he thought he could choose not to kill himself for at least one month to give him and the therapist a chance to see whether there was enough about his life he could like in order to choose to stay alive. He was asked to make a "no suicide" contract (Weishaar & Beck, 1990). He said he could delay killing himself. Had there been an ambivalent or negative response, one of two interventions would have been employed. The therapist would have inquired as to whether he could keep himself alive one week, or three days, or until the next day at 10:00 a.m. If he could not guarantee to stay alive until the next day, the parents would have been told to take him to a hospital for admission when they left the therapist's office.

Sometimes parents or the spouse of a depressed person are reluctant or unwilling to hospitalize a member of the family, especially if the depressed individual refuses hospitalization or threatens to kill himself if he/she is put in the hospital. If the therapist cannot negotiate a "no suicide" contract or effect an immediate hospitalization, then a "suicide watch" can be instituted. A "suicide watch" means that someone is awake and keeping watch over the suicidal individual 24 hours a day. Careful vigilance is prescribed and described. For example, if the watcher needs to use the bathroom, someone else must assume the watch. If the suicidal individual needs to use the bathroom, he/she must be accompanied. The suicidal person must *never* be left alone. Sometimes it is necessary to involve extended family if the watch must continue for more than a few days.

The assessment method suggested above, the acknowledgment of personal strengths, the "no suicide" contract, and "suicide watch" interventions can be used by the clergy depending on their experience and training and their comfort dealing with suicidal depressed individuals. For those not trained or comfortable, referral to a mental health professional trained to deal with severe depression should be made as soon as possible. These professionals include pastoral therapists, clinical psychologists, clinical social workers, and psychiatrists.

References

Beck AT, Rush AJ, Shaw BF, Emery G: *Cognitive Therapy of Depression.* New York, Guilford Press, 1979.

Black DW, Winokur G: Suicide and psychiatric diagnosis. In Blumenthal SJ, Kupfer DJ (editors): *Suicide Over the Life Cycle: Risk Factors, Assessment, and Treatment of Suicidal Patients.* Washington, DC, American Psychiatric Press Inc., 1990, pages 135-153.

Duke MP, Nowicki S: Theories of personality and psychopathology: Schools derived from psychology and philosophy. In Kaplan HI, Sadock BJ (editors): *Comprehensive Textbook of Psychiatry / V. 5th edition.* Baltimore, MD, Williams and Wilkins, 1989, 1: 432-448.

Rogers CR, Sanford RC: Client-centered psychotherapy. In Kaplan HI, Sadock BJ (editors): *Comprehensive Textbook of Psychiatry / V. 5th edition.* Baltimore, MD, Williams and Wilkins, 1989, 2: 1482-1501.

Weishaar ME, Beck AT: Cognitive approaches to understanding and treating suicidal behavior. In Blumenthal SJ, Kupfer DJ (editors): *Suicide Over the Life Cycle: Risk Factors, Assessment, and Treatment of Suicidal Patients.* Washington, DC, American Psychiatric Press Inc., 1990, pages 469-498.

Chapter 6

How to Get Professional Help for a Suicidal Person and Remain Involved

**Thomas Jobe, M.D.,
Rev. James H. Shackelford, Ph.D.,
and Rev. Dan G. Stauffacher, D.Min.**

Introduction

The authors begin by presenting three separate views of how to handle a common problem: getting help for the suicidal person and staying involved. It is easy to run into problems when trying to get help for someone. It is equally easy to refer someone (once a resource is found) and then forget about them. Good pastoral care tries to be alert to needs, aware of resources, and available for continued contact after the referral has been made.

Dr. Jobe outlines four problems that may be encountered when making referrals into the mental health system and offers suggestions for handling each. Rev. Shackelford warns us not be alarmed when our referral plans go awry — we should *expect* that nothing will go as planned—and reviews the kinds of issues that arise when we try to help a suicidal person engage in treatment. Finally, Rev. Stauffacher focuses on practical skills inherent to the clergy, unique qualities of pastoral care, and a step-by-step technique for success in the face of predictable difficulties accessing help or making referrals.

Problems typically encountered when making referrals — Dr. Jobe

There are four broad problem areas that arise when referring persons with suicidal impulses or feelings to a mental health professional. First, an individual's type of insurance coverage constrains what sort of help he/she will receive. Secondly, some persons in acute need refuse mental health assistance and some of these may need to be hospitalized involuntarily. Third, some persons with suicidal symptoms also exhibit plausible-sounding delusions; in these cases the suicidal feelings occasionally appear to be extreme but otherwise normal reactions to stressful life situations. The final problem facing clergy dealing with suicidal parishioners is that some suicidal persons decide to quit psychotherapy or stop taking the medication prescribed for their particular illness without informing family members or therapists.

When making a referral for mental health care, one must be aware of the importance of the person's insurance coverage for choosing varying types and qualities of care. There has been a major economic shift in the U.S. toward managed care plans in recent years. Therefore it is important not only to know the parishioner's type of insurance plan, but also the identity of the primary contact person for that plan. When making a referral, someone should take responsibility to check with the relevant insurance company to determine whether the person belongs to a Health Maintenance Organization (HMO), and whether or not he/she is already seeing a mental health professional. Either the clergyperson, a family member, or the patient should maintain continued contact with the insurance triage person at the HMO to confirm payment for subsequent mental health care visits. If these steps are not taken, a patient may incur unreimbursed expenses which could later engender resistance to further treatment. If there is no insurance, mandated care is available through publicly funded programs, but access often requires special effort on the part of some interested party.

While it is good to be vigilant about problems that require immediate attention, sometimes the potential patient will become frightened when the pastor says he/she needs to be seen by someone *today* — it may make him/her more upset and may further accelerate anxiety and resistance to treatment. If there is any danger that the person may harm him/herself or others, or that the person cannot adequately care for his/her own physical needs anymore, then the Mental Health Code of most states requires that the person be admitted for inpatient care for protection of self and others. If the person is not willing to admit him/herself, the process of involuntary admission is a complicated one but often necessary. Clergypersons or any lay person can petition the police to take a person to an emergency room for a mental health evaluation. Only a psychiatrist and certain other designated mental health professionals, however, have the legal authority to certify someone as in need of involuntary hospitalization for a period of observation and treatment. Thus involuntary hospitalization is only possible when a legally empowered mental health professional completes a face-to-face examination and concludes the patient is either incapable of caring for him/herself or a possible harm to self or others. In Illinois, for example, certifying someone to inpatient care mandates that he/she remain in the hospital for a five-day examination period. After this time has lapsed, only a court has the authority to decide the patient needs to remain in the hospital for a longer period of time, i.e., commitment of sixty days or longer.

Two problems commonly arise from the system of arranging involuntary hospitalization. The first is the legal nature of the process itself. Clergy must be linked to mental health professionals in order to make certain that their parishioners will be properly cared for. The ideal, particularly in smaller communities, is for the pastor to identify one familiar mental health professional with whom he/she has worked well in the past, someone the pastor can refer a parishioner to for assessment or treatment. A thorough one-session diagnostic examination is not prohibitively expensive, and often produces a clear picture of recommended choices or alternatives. The examiner may also uncover other details that would not normally be known to and/or discovered by clergy — additional data which may ultimately affect treatment decisions such as the existence of physical, sexual, or psychological abuse.

The other problem is that the examining psychiatrist may not be willing to certify that the patient requires hospitalization, based on the information the patient presents to him/her. Mental health professionals vary in their degree of willingness to certify patients for involuntary hospital commitment. The key to making an accurate judgment is having detailed information. In a suicidal crisis, the clergyperson and family should not feel like they are violating privacy or confidence by providing the mental health professional with all the information they have. This kind of information often proves to be invaluable in making a proper assessment of the crisis severity.

Another resistance to referring people to mental health care is because clergy and family members may fail to recognize mental illness amidst the person's other problems. *Delusional depression* is one illness wherein the person's symptoms make it difficult to properly assess the severity of illness. Delusions are ideas accompanied by intense feelings that often have a kind of plausibility to them; they may not be at all bizarre. People experiencing delusional depression often appear to have normal emotional reactions to the situations they describe. The delusions can be a very serious issue in major depressive illness, particularly if the delusions are connected to suicidal ideation. Delusions should be viewed as foreboding very serious consequences.

For example, a patient who was brought to the hospital emergency room (ER) by a co-worker reported he had run over a small child, leaving a dent in the fender of his company car. He became so frightened he left the scene of the accident and now felt overwhelmed by guilt. He came to the ER because he felt he should turn himself in to the authorities as the perpetrator of a hit-and-run accident. The person was otherwise very coherent. But at this point, the co-worker reported that he (the co-worker) had put the same dent in the fender on another company trip; the dent had nothing to do with hitting a child. The patient was subsequently admitted to an inpatient unit for treatment. His family visited him that day, and after they left the patient took a pair of scissors into the bathroom and stabbed himself in the chest several times. Thankfully, the patient survived. When he was interviewed later about the stabbing incident, the patient explained that he had become (erroneously) convinced that after his family left that night, they would never return because of his crime. The convictions of this patient fostered tremendous feelings of guilt, remorse and anxiety.

Fluctuating delusional states as well as auditory hallucinations are very serious symptoms of depressive and other illnesses, and will often be the first manifestation of illness visible to clergy. For this reason, clergy and family members of depressed people should be suspicious of deeply held convictions which come on suddenly. It may be tempting to not notice or acknowledge the mentally ill nature of this type of behavior because of the situation's plausibility. But because of the potentially grave consequences of this behavior, it must be viewed with the highest level of caution.

The final problem facing a clergyperson when making a referral is that some psychiatric patients remove themselves from treatment and/or go off their medication when they become most acutely ill. When faced with a psychiatric patient who is not compliant with part or all of his/her treatment program, the clergy should try to develop rapport with the patient and obtain permission to talk to his/her psychiatrist and family. Then the clergy can act as an advocate to bring the person back into compliance with the treatment program. Non-compliant or help-refusing patients usually have a high degree of denial. Sometimes, because of a family secret, family members conspire in the patient's denial process. Patients often do not believe they need their medication, so they simply do not take it. In these cases, it is important to coordinate an orchestrated response from all those involved in helping so a team approach can be taken to get the person back in treatment.

Connecting a person with a caregiver is best done by developing relationships with both the parishioner and the potential mental health care provider, by remaining alert to the serious aspects of life crises, and by being a vocal advocate for mental health concerns to diminish the social stigma of mental illness. By following through with support and advocacy on behalf of parishioners, it is more than possible to connect them with the care they need.

Practical lessons for getting help — Rev. Shackleford

One of the things that we need to think about, when we talk about getting professional help for a suicidal person, is the context and community in which we live and in which we have our church. Each context is different. Medical, hospital and mental health resources vary greatly from one community to the next. In what follows, the pastor will need to apply what is said to the specific context in which he/she ministers. I will focus on the practicalities of getting professional help for suicidal persons to whom the pastor is ministering. First I will comment about the various standards of care that may apply.

Nally vs. Grace Community Church (1988) is an important court case in California that raised questions about what standards of care should apply to pastors. The Nally family sued the Grace Community Church and its pastors for failing to refer properly a suicidal man who had come to them seeking spiritual counsel and who subsequently committed suicide. The case has gone through the appeals process. The California Appeals court decided that pastors were not to be held to the same standards of care as other mental health professionals. So regardless of whether or not they referred him to a mental health professional, they could not be found liable for Mr. Nally's death. In fact, they had referred him to a psychologist, but he never went to see the psychologist. Legally, according to this and similar cases, pastors are not subject to mental health care laws. However, if the pastor explicitly offers "counseling" and is explicitly viewed as a "counselor," he/she would be subject to the same standards of care as a mental health professional. The Nally decision is important in placing what pastors do within the larger professional communities in which we function. In spite of the Nally decision, I believe that pastors should follow the highest standards of care when it comes to responding to suicidal parishioners. We should consistently look after the best interests of our parishioners and take positive actions to help these folk receive help.

When thinking of the practical issues of getting a parishioner to mental health care, one must face certain limitations. Referrals are always limited by what is available, how the mental health system responds, whether people choose to stay in the system once referred, whether there are alternative treatment choices, and whether their health insurance covers the cost of treatment. As both a pastor and a professional, knowing what to do for a parishioner in crisis and knowing how much is enough are huge burdens.

In the church, the confessional with its corollary privilege of confidential communication is deep-seated. We have been taught that whatever is confessed to us as pastors should remain private. However, our culture says that sometimes we must do more than listen in response to a confession. If someone is going to hurt him/herself or others, secular law dictates that we have a duty to step out from behind our confessional role and try to protect those endangered. I believe this is not just a secular duty but a spiritual duty as well. Life is sacred. We are called to invite all to choose life, not death. We may be witnesses to tragedy if we do not act to protect. The key is to learn to balance respect for our parishioners' privacy with our responsibility for their safety. This is no easy task. It's a matter of judgment and concerned involvement with our parishioners.

If persons are able to protect themselves, we must not do it for them. If they will call, make an appointment with a psychiatrist, walk themselves over to the emergency room, or if their family will go with them to the emergency room, we should encourage them to do so. In these cases, it is our role to stand by and be a supportive presence, making sure things do not fall through the cracks. As long as a person feels in charge and is able to say "I need help," their situation is *prognostically* better. As pastors, we must recognize the limitations of our role as supporter and facilitator. We can help empower the person to care for him/herself. We can help mobilize his/her support system. We can help the person find the appropriate professional help. However, there is often a temptation to go past our own limits and over-extend ourselves.

Whenever possible, it is wise to involve other people in the decisions about next steps and treatment alternatives. Decisions should not be made in isolation. If there is a family or supportive people are available, use them to help in the situation. Support networks that can be called upon should not be ignored, because they can be a great resource. If professionals in the community can be called upon, use them as well. This means developing a ministry network that includes relationships with psychiatrists, psychologists, the emergency room, as well as other counseling resources. Functioning in isolation is one of the greatest risks of ministry. Responding to the threat of suicide is not something pastors should do alone.

Whether it is better to over-respond or under-respond is a tricky question. I think there is a general tendency to over-respond. My basic principle for intervention is that one should do the *least* one can do and be able to reasonably believe that parishioners will receive needed help. Each situation is a judgment call. Real risks do exist. When there is no question the person is suicidal, he/she should be taken directly to the emergency room. The Hillburten Act, the current law in the U.S., states that emergency rooms must responsibly treat, hospitalize, or transfer to an appropriate facility those patients who seek help regardless of their ability to pay. Thus, the emergency room becomes the first backup when people are in acute crisis, and when we fear they are unable to take care of themselves or may harm themselves or others.

A number of problems arise once a referral is made and even after treatment has begun. Awareness of these issues may help the pastor prevent their occurrence. The problems involve what sort of therapy is recommended, the length of time therapy takes to become effective, payment for treatment, and premature discharge from hospitalization.

Referrals can be made to private therapists, but sometimes they cannot see patients for several weeks and are unavailable for emergency assessments. Problems about ability to pay for therapists' services may also arise. For these reasons, it is important to develop personal relationships with professionals — especially psychiatrists and physicians — so that the pastor can be confident that they will respond when he/she needs to call upon them for help in a crisis. It is equally important to develop good rapport with clinics, hospitals and emergency rooms, so the pastor becomes aware of how they work and how they can be used when crises occur.

Clergy should not expect anything to work the way it should. If a pastor gives a phone number for a parishioner in need to call, the pastor should make sure to follow-up to be certain the parishioner actually calls. Pastors should be sure referral resources are available and not on vacation. If a referral can fall through a crack, it will. If the pastor refers someone to the emergency room, he/she should have someone escort the person there. This person could be a family member, the pastor, or even the police. More than one escort is preferable because being in the car with someone who is very upset can be dangerous. Be practical and get the help needed to safely transport someone to an emergency room.

In therapy, antidepressant medications often take three to six weeks to become effective. They are not quick cures. The treating physician may need to try several different medications in serial fashion before finally lighting on one that has the desired impact. Anti-anxiety medications — used when there is agitation, panic attacks, or "high anxiety" — are effective faster. In either case, do not expect medications to work quickly. Be aware that sometimes the risk of suicide increases when medications begin to work, because energy levels increase while the person is still depressed. There is an increased risk of suicide after two weeks on an antidepressant medication. Keeping in touch with parishioners and their families after help is received and medications are begun is important for this reason. Education about medication and consistent follow-up visits with treating professionals should be stressed. One cannot assume that compliance with the recommended treatment occurs naturally.

In the same vein, psychotherapy should not be expected to work quickly either. Psychotherapy takes time. Reactive depressions often respond to therapy within three months of weekly sessions. This can be a rocky time for the depressed person. Talking through problems does help. Talking to pastors helps a lot. But talking to a mental health professional often allows a person to discuss issues that may be too private to share with a pastor who knows him/her in multiple contexts. In situations like these, psychotherapy may be the best, albeit not the fastest solution. Depressions that are more deep-seated may require verbal therapy over a period of months or even years.

Do not expect insurance to pay in full or even at all for mental health care. Our society is reaching a crisis in health care. Insurance companies no longer want to pay for mental health and substance abuse treatment. Many insurance carriers are limiting coverage for mental health services to crisis intervention only. Some policies will only cover treatment of substance abuse once or twice in a person's lifetime, and substance abusers are high risk candidates for suicide. The insurance situation in this country can make getting treatment for these persons very difficult. Alliances with professionals and medical facilities who provide care at a discounted cost are important.

Finally, when someone is brought to the emergency room for an evaluation, the pastor may be faced with the need to petition for their involuntary admission. It is always best to try to have the person request hospitalization, thereby voluntarily admitting him/herself. However, if the person resists the idea, working with the emergency room staff to request their admission may become necessary. The three grounds for involuntary admission are as follows: the person is likely to injure him/herself, the person is likely to injure others, or the person is unable to care for him/herself due to a mental illness. The pastor may need to be the petitioner, but only a physician can legally certify the need for structured care and hospitalization. If these conditions apply and the process is successful, the person can be admitted to hospital care involuntarily. However, the patient still has the right to refuse treatment and to ask for discharge. When the patient requests a discharge, the hospital must petition a court to detain him/her within the next five working days, or the hospital is required to discharge the person. Thus, even if all the correct steps are taken, the pastor may still find the person back in his/her study and not in mental health care. The pastor needs to be aware of their internal irritations at their parishioners and at the health care system when this happens. The pastor needs to set aside these reactions and respond to the parishioner's needs.

It would be idyllic to be able to refer a person for treatment and have the mental health care system take over smoothly from that point. Unfortunately, that is not the way it always works. It is often much more complicated. *The system is fallible.* Therefore, the pastor's role is to be the guardian of the process, being sure persons do not get dropped by treatment or forgotten. Even if it takes several attempts to get a person effective treatment, it is ultimately worth the effort.

The unique position and qualities of the pastor — Rev. Stauffacher

As clergy, we have unique skills and tools that we can offer to people, ones that are different from those offered by physicians and other caregivers. Because we deal with our parishioners on a more personal level than mental health professionals, our relationship with them is a more intimate one. We know their families and friends and often even their particular family history. We are "general practitioners" who still have the capacity to visit folk where they live and work. The use of this sort of visit is one of the primary abilities that sets us apart from other caregivers in the quality of care we can give to people and our special ability to remain involved.

A second tool available to clergy caregivers is *pastoral truth*. While it is important that clergy not say things that will damage folk, it is equally important that clergy say things of substance. Well-worn clichés or rehearsed formula answers are not helpful when given as responses to serious questions about life. Simply telling someone that "things will be better with time" or "you're handling this quite well" may be fine as openers to a conversation, but these phrases are not of enough substance in and of themselves to offer any help. We are challenged, as clergy, to see the truth, speak the truth, and live the truth. Anything else may be our own form of denial. Denial can lead us to become accomplices to the lie that the person is not really in grave danger of killing him/herself. We must try to see the situation as clearly as possible.

Our third tool as pastoral caregivers is to practice what we preach — be honest and open. The work of pastoral care in psychiatric illness differs from the work of other mental health care professionals, because we do not have the secular skills necessary to "treat" the person, nor do we have the statistics and diagnostic information to speak as experts on the topic. The real tool we have can be called down-to-earth practicality, i.e., "Tom, your life as you tell me about it sounds and feels very conflicted at this time and I recommend you talk to a doctor about it." The pastor might also suggest talking to the person's family. One may also ask permission to obtain a consultation from a doctor one knows, trusts, and has worked with before, or even offer to take the person to a doctor for an evaluation.

As pastors of local churches (or wherever we serve), we are not in the business of replacing caregiving facilities within the community. It is our job to know what those resources are, to know where they are, and to form a relationship with them so that a contact or referral can be made when necessary. The time to make provision for this piece of pastoral care is before it is needed. The worst time to try and make these kinds of contacts is in the midst of a crisis. Bridges are not built in crisis moments. If the pastor believes that a person may be suicidal, it is sometimes helpful to ask him/her about that possibility. Once this belief is confirmed, the pastor can connect him/her with a professional who is competent to handle the person's particular issues.

A list of different mental health resources can be developed in a variety of ways. Clergy can talk to other clergy in the same area and find out who they work with when faced with a depressed, possibly suicidal parishioner. Pastors should inform themselves about the public mental health offices in their area and visit them to learn about their services and procedures. Pastors should ask their own family physician to whom he/she refer clients. One can also respond to some of the mailings received from private practitioners. Use the local hospital physician referral service. Some pastors find it valuable to call the local schools and ask a social worker, guidance counselor, or administrator who they have had contact with in the past and who would be chosen if the school needed to make a referral. Finally, one can always ask some parishioners who they know and respect in the mental health field.

Once the pastor has this initial information, the next step is to call each of the possibilities and "interview" them politely and gently. The pastor should explain why he/she is calling and try to ascertain as much information from them as possible. In a crisis, the name and phone number of the person to contact should be easily accessible. Inquire what the person's area of expertise/specialty is. Find out if he/she works with depressed, suicidal people and if there are certain types of cases he/she will not handle. Find out if there is a best time to call and whether or not he/she handles emergencies. Ask if his/her answering service calls the mental health professional directly or if the service waits for him/her to call in for messages. The customary payment structure is very important information to ascertain — i.e., if third party payment (insurance) is accepted or whether private payment is necessary, if public aid of any kind is accepted, and whether there is a fixed rate or a sliding scale. It may also be useful to be aware of general office/patient hours. If necessary, will the mental health professional provide a one-time consultation/evaluation, and is there a fee for this? Also inquire as to whether he/she works alone or in a group practice. It is particularly useful to write all these important points down and keep them in an accessible place for the moment of need.

Good mental health care, especially in the case of depression and possible suicide, does not happen in a single bold stroke where magic pills solve everything by tomorrow. It all takes time. Some antidepressant medications take several weeks to build up to therapeutic levels in the bloodstream and body of a depressed individual. As pastoral caregivers, we can be supportive of this and also be observant for changes when they occur. This is the time when our particular tools and skills as clergy are important. The technique here is to make brief visits (phone or home) from time to time while the person is in treatment, after a hospitalization (if there was one), as well as after the end of formal treatment.

Getting good professional help for a depressed and suicidal person is difficult. Both Drs. Jobe and Shackleford have reminded us that nothing goes quite as hoped and planned. There are external realities over which we have no control (funding, hospital bed availability, patient cooperation, etc.). Staying involved, however, is not so contingent on external forces. Staying involved is to a great extent a function of our care for the person and our ability to be self-initiating in efforts to journey with him/her back to health.

Chapter 7

Supporting the Family of a Suicidal Person: Those Who Live in Fear

John T. Maltsberger, M.D.,
Thomas Jobe, M.D., and
Rev. Dan G. Stauffacher, D.Min.

In this chapter, the authors discuss the case of Sally and how her family responded to her seven-year experience with depression and suicidal behavior. Sally's case has been altered somewhat to protect her identity and that of her family. These changes of name and location do not affect the content of the case. The truth is, many of us know a "Sally" at some time in our ministries.

As we look at this case, keep in mind that our focus here is giving support to Sally's family. Sally clearly had quite a serious problem. What can we do, as clergy, to help her family?

I. The case of Sally

Sally died three weeks short of her twenty-second birthday. At her funeral her father approached the pastor and said, "I don't know if I should be grieving, sad, and crying now — or relieved and thankful. It's been so long and painful these last seven years." Sally had attempted suicide the first time when she was fifteen (sophomore year in high school). Unknown to her parents, she had been feeling "out of sorts" for some time and talked with her girlfriend about "ending it all" on several occasions. The usual reply was, "... oh Sally, you don't mean it." She cut her wrists that time.

In the emergency room she received five or six stitches in each wrist and was referred to the county mental health department. After a couple of counseling sessions her parents were told that her attempted suicide was not serious. It was only an episode of acting out to get attention. Her parents' concern turned to anger as they wondered, "How could she do this?!"

Her second attempt came in her senior year. This time she took pills from the medicine cabinet at a friend's house and almost died. She was found by her brother. Paramedics were called — ambulance, emergency room and three weeks in an inpatient adolescent psychiatric unit followed. She came home with a prescription for antidepressant medication and regular appointments at the county mental health department. With treatment, her up-and-down moods leveled out and her grades improved slightly, but she never rejoined all the school activities that once had been an important part of her life.

When college time came, she elected to go to the local community college. During her two years there she had another serious episode of depression, but no suicide attempt. Her doctor and therapist were able to help with antidepressant medication and supportive weekly psychotherapy sessions. This time, she also participated in outpatient group therapy. Her parents and older brother worried about her all the time. Her mood swings sent them into mood swings of their own. They feared what would happen if she transferred to an out-of-town college.

Sally also feared leaving her hometown support network and so stayed out of school for a year after completing two years at community college. Her moods leveled out and she began to feel good about herself again. She felt like she knew her problem and could handle whatever might happen. So she went off to finish college at a school about three hours' drive away from home. The first semester was uneventful and Christmas with the family was one of the best ever. It was great to see Sally happy again.

March came. Sally was coming home for Spring break. The family was looking forward to it. When Mom returned home from a trip to the grocery store, she saw Sally's car in front of the house. Moments later she found Sally in the basement. She had hung herself. Mom's first words were, "If only I had stayed home and not gone shopping..." Dad was silent. Her older brother cried and sat alone in the garage.

II. General reflections — Dr. Jobe

The father really sets the tone for this case in his opening words. He knew his feelings were complex, but he reports confusion about what he "should" feel. His choice of the word "should" is interesting but not unusual. It hints at the notion of there being a correct or appropriate emotional response, rather than owning up to and dealing with what he is really feeling. It is sometimes observed that when someone is looking for what he or she "should" feel, the person is also hinting at his/her own denial or ambivalence.

Therapeutically, there is much that could have been done for Sally, not the least of which was involving the family in counseling, support groups, self-help groups, or individual counseling. Had Sally been diagnosed with diabetes, it is a good guess that the parents and siblings would have taken steps to read about and understand the problem. They would have made adjustments in their lifestyles and gone on to live a modified but nonetheless full life with Sally. In Sally's case, though, nothing is said about any support groups or education about depression for anyone. Like many illnesses and psychological problems, support for both the patient and the primary social group around the patient can be very helpful.

The family's shock at the first suicide attempt is not unusual. Frequently a teenager will talk to friends more than to family, and when a suicide attempt is made the unexpectedness of it is almost overwhelming. In these circumstances, shock and anger are understandable responses.

What is problematic about the period following the first attempt is that the caregiving facilities seem to have misjudged the situation. Her case was referred to an outpatient county facility where her attempt was passed off as inconsequential and not indicative of a major psychiatric illness. Many cases of depression can be and are handled quite well in outpatient settings, both public and private. However, in this case, the deeper signs of a troubled young lady may have been missed. The parents' responses turned from concern to anger, but they were still unable to appreciate Sally's mood swings as evidence of a major emotional disorder.

Her second attempted suicide was a life-threatening overdose of some unknown medicine. In some cases, the only difference between an attempted and completed suicide is the medical consequences of the act. An overdose of this type is very serious, and it appears to have been sheer fortune that the brother found her when he did.

It is appropriate to inquire here about two very fundamental issues: (a) Has Sally been informed of and accepted her emotional disorder? and (b) Have the family members been informed of and accepted her emotional disorder? Is there a psychological, sexual, and/or physical abuse history in this family? Nothing in the vignette gives any answer to these questions. However, we do get the impression that the family is inextricably involved with Sally's episodes, mood swings, and emotional disorder. Good pastoral care at this point might simply be to ask these questions and perhaps even link the family with self-help or support groups in their area that deal with depression and suicide. There are a broad range of professionally-led as well as self-help groups that can help with the ups and downs the family experiences and also help with fears that may be present regarding the disclosure of family "secrets" and reconciliation of family members.

The vignette continues with Sally's family following her movements through life. Nothing is said about anything done for them to help alleviate the stress in their lives. Nor is anything said directly about how they handle their feelings and emotions — until the very end. Mom feels guilt for the suicide that could have been prevented if only she had been more aware of Sally's mental state. Dad is silent. The question one might ask here is: is this the way he handles his emotions all the time — with silence, holding them in? The older brother cries alone in the garage. The crying is a healthy response and a way to begin the grieving process. The fact that he is alone in the garage is somewhat problematic, and raises the questions about whether or not this is the way the family communicates, through isolation and aloneness.

III. Effects on the family — Dr. Maltsberger

It is impossible to live for a prolonged period of time with someone like Sally who has serious depressive illness, and especially someone who is intermittently suicidal, without being affected. Frequently the feeling becomes one of profound helplessness. In this case, the parents and brother worried about Sally all the time, and her mood swings sent them into ups and downs.

This sense of helplessness can become so intense that it is advisable to recommend counseling for the family from the very beginning to help support them in a number of ways:

(a) To help them understand more about the illness affecting them directly or indirectly;

(b) To help them sort out their styles of communication and hopefully to improve them;

(c) To help them with feelings of helplessness;

(d) To help them with feelings of anger and hate;

(e) To help them avoid the trap of grandiosity, that is, thinking they can work a miracle on their own; and

(f) To help them with forgiveness and the grieving process if necessary.

Too often counseling and support is given or offered to a family dealing with a major depressive illness as a last resort. By that time, the situation is so serious that any prognosis is guarded.

The type of depressive illness that Sally had, as described in the vignette, is clearly chronic. Before her suicide there had been seven years of ups and downs with and without medication, with and without therapy, with good times and bad. A family going through this type of turmoil is bound to develop feelings of anger and hate. The vignette makes note of this.

The anger in dealing with chronic illness is sometimes preconscious and sometimes unconscious. In the case of suicidal threatening, it can be doubled and re-doubled, affecting not only the family, but also psychiatrists, social workers, pastoral counselors, pastors, friends, and a host of other people who come into contact with the person. Anger is like stormy weather: if all the conditions are there, a storm will happen and there is no controlling it. People cannot turn anger on and off by an act of will — there is no light switch for anger. Acknowledging it is the first step toward handling it.

The anger in dealing with chronic depressive illness where the possibility of suicide looms great comes from the human response to a life of daily uncertainty. When someone you love is constantly threatening to abandon you, never to see you anymore, and could do it at almost any time, it generates terrible feelings of anger at some level. This anger may be expressed in any combination of the following:

(a) **Denial** — the importance of communications and behaviors are overlooked, ignored, or discounted. At some level we say, "this is not happening, I am not hearing what I am hearing, I am not seeing what I am seeing, what is happening is not real." Denial can lead us into riding the emotional ups and downs with the person without really understanding why or what is going on.

(b) **Paralysis** — in the presence of daily uncertainty, never knowing for sure what is really happening with someone, a low-grade sense of panic about what to do can develop that leads to a feeling of needing to be perfect in what we do and how we respond. We say to ourselves, "just as soon as I/we get the right answers, everything will be all right." Waiting for the right (perfect) answers leads us to pain, causing anger that immobilizes or paralyzes us.

(c) **Overt anger** — "I'm so exhausted and worn out with your suicidal threatening. If you are going to do it, I wish to God you would go on and get it over with. I cannot go on like this any more."

(d) **Reaction formation** — when the family cannot deal with the reality of the situation and cannot tolerate their increasing anger toward the chronically depressed person, they labor hard to keep their feelings buried quite deeply. What comes out is a sugar sweetness, the sugar of arsenic: "And how are we feeling this morning, dear? You don't feel like killing yourself this morning, do you?"

(e) **Guilt** — whatever happens is my/our fault. Hidden here is also the taint of grandiosity that somehow what I/we did is the sole cause (or at least the primary cause) of the suicide.

The thought of a major psychiatric illness having a part in the suicide does not enter into the situation. Neither do the responsibility and decisions of the patient enter into consideration.

Families can and do sometimes tear themselves to pieces over an illness like this. One of the greatest challenges for clergy working with these families is to be aware of the problems, especially the problem of anger and the problems with anger. When evidence of anger is seen, it is important to give some sort of helpful interpretation. Sometimes it cannot be done immediately. There are people who could not stand it if one were to point out to them how furious they must be with "Sally."

When faced with an angry family, the pastor should look for a "pastoral moment" when he/she might say something like, "How terribly stressful it is to live with someone like this. What are you doing for yourself to keep going? It takes the patience of a saint for you to live in a circumstance like this." With that kind of support, they may confess that Sally is just a little hard to take.

IV. What support clergy bring to the family system — Rev. Stauffacher

Dr. Peggy Way of Eden Theological Seminary often says, "Pastoral care in the local church is always messy and dangerous personally, politically and economically." It is, however, *more* dangerous not to provide good pastoral care. At the least, when facing any given situation, honesty must prevail, even when that honesty is to say we don't know what to do. To see something potentially harmful or dangerous and not do anything about it is a poor form of pastoral care. Enmeshed with denial, it only promotes the problem. Not helping folk to see and deal with reality does not help the healing.

In supporting the family of a suicidal person, we must first recognize that they do live under constant fear. It is not something that can be resolved with a quick-fix prayer. It will not go away if we ignore it, and it cannot be blamed on the devil. Research is going on in various parts of our country that suggests the possibility of a genetic predisposition to major depressive illness. If that is the case, the illness becomes an issue of creation, not temptation. That is the work of God and not anyone else.

What we as clergy bring to a family like Sally's is our genuineness and our vulnerability. We bring our capacity to stand with them amid their fear and apart from them in a position of objectivity. We are priest, rabbi, prophet, pastor and everything in between. We bring what the secular world does not bring. We bring testament, sacrament, covenant, and community.

In the best of experiences, we can be an active part of the treatment team dealing with the overall issue of the depressive illness and its effects not only on the identified patient, but also on the family. We are not a cheap replacement for good medical and psychological care in our communities, nor are we the omniscient judge of right and wrong, good and bad, health and illness.

We are called to stand among people and with people. When a family within our community needs support, we are often the first ones called. Sadly, especially in the cause of a completed suicide, we are called to be among those who help with the rituals of saying good-bye. We spend a lot of time reflecting and interpreting reality in the hope that it will facilitate wholeness and healing. In doing this, the first and most important kind of support we can bring to a family like Sally's is our own maturity, accountability, and health.

We need to be mature enough to know what we can handle and what we cannot. We also need to be mature enough to see the truth and speak the truth with compassion. Dr. Maltsberger's piece in this chapter expresses this quite well. Our accountability is to our faith, our faith community, our professional peers and colleagues, and ourselves. To forsake any of these is serious and weakens the support we can bring to a family like Sally's.

Health is critical: mental health, spiritual health, and physical health. It would seem hypocritical of us to offer counseling and pastoral care to anyone if we have not first experienced it and received it ourselves. We do not have to experience every kind of pain to know pain. We do, however, need to experience our own pain in order to stand with Sally's family and acknowledge their pain, anger, or whatever. Then, like the metaphorical shepherds, we can guide them out of it — from the valley of despair and pain, to the green pastures where a table is set before them in the presence of the enemies known as denial, unhealthy paralyzing emotions, isolation, and scripted programmed responses. Healing can and does happen in this context.

Both Drs. Jobe and Maltsberger have observed in this chapter that Sally's family did not seem to deal with emotions and communication very well. Assuming they were active in a faith community, pastoral care and support take the form of helping them deal with these issues. More likely, it would involve the process of raising their awareness to these problems and then helping them into some kind of structured experience where they can begin to do the necessary work. This could be family therapy, individual therapy, a support group, or a self-help group. Notice that all these ways of support involve the active presence of "another." Support and care always happen in the context of a community. I have never experienced support in a vacuum.

In supporting a family like Sally's, we cannot take away the constant fear, but we can help it. After we have brought the resources of our faith, education is the next strength and support we can offer. Reading this book is a great start. From here, follow up with competent professionals in the local community to develop collegial review and referral sources.

Elsewhere in this volume (see Chapter 4 on "Recognizing Suicidal Risk") I have listed several skills available to clergy for recognizing suicidal risk. Those same skills are also valuable in providing support to families living under the constant fear of suicide. We all know that early recognition is the best treatment of anything. Using these skills of recognition to provide support bridges a gap between illness and wellness. Of all those skills — home visitor, spiritual caregiver, being pastoral not secular in our care/support-giving, educator, advocate for health, referral-maker, tolerant, variable in the amount of care/support given, recognizing from whence our authority comes, forgiveness, and a conduit of the divine — one stands out as the most important... Have courage.

Have courage to see the truth, live the truth, and speak the truth in love. The truth, reality, is the greatest support available. It holds no surprises. It is as it is and affords to us the opportunity to grow and be strong. As clergy, we are one part of a healing treatment team that can speak the truth in faith and compassion. We can help gather people around the truth for healing, growth, and support.

Chapter 8

Confidentiality and Expressed Suicide Intent

Laurel Arthur Burton, Th.D.

Introduction

Clergy are positioned at a unique and privileged conjunction of human relationships: they listen to personal stories seldom intended for public hearing while representing the common life of the faith community. From time to time, therefore, clergy are privy to communications that thrust them into moral quandaries as they mediate between the value claims of the individual and the community.

It is relatively clear, from a legal standpoint at least, that clergy have a "duty to warn" in the event they learn about an intention to harm another person, even if it means breaking the bonds of a pastoral confidence. There is, however, less clarity about clergy's obligation to speak or remain silent about a congregant's expressed intent to commit suicide or otherwise harm himself. The following case illustration is adapted from one written by the Reverend Fr. James Corrigan, OSA, who specializes in AIDS pastoral care and education.

The case of Mr. S who has AIDS

Mr. S, a person with AIDS, is a member of Rev. K's congregation. Mr. S was first diagnosed with a form of pneumonia commonly associated with AIDS and then with Kaposi's Sarcoma, a form of cancer also found mostly in people with AIDS. He was recently admitted to the hospital with end-stage disease and in great pain due to pancreatitis. When she visits the hospital, Rev. K is aware that there are plans to discharge Mr. S to home hospice in several days.

During Rev. K's visits with Mr. S in the hospital, Mr. S states that he is really not interested in hospice because he and his friends have a plan to end his life. When asked for specifics, Mr. S declines to discuss matters any further except to state that the quality of his life is an issue for him, and that he has discussed this with his mother. He reports that although his mother was upset at first, she has since concluded that he knows best. Rev. K left the hospital saying that she was concerned about him and needed to think further about their conversation. Mr. S stated that he wanted their conversation to be held in confidence.

After consulting with a psychiatrist, Rev. K returned to see Mr. S and told him that she did not agree with his intended action. She shared with him that she had heard of other people with AIDS who at one time may have had these feelings and who had then changed their minds and sought help. After receiving help, she said, they were often relieved that they did not end their lives as they had originally wanted.

The next day, while Mr. S was still on the unit, a hospice nurse (without any knowledge of the above conversation) visited with the patient, who agreed to hospice. His discharge was consequently delayed in order to set up the hospice plans. When Rev. K learned of this delay and the reason for it, she thought that Mr. S might have had a change of heart and returned to talk. Mr. S reaffirmed his plans to end his life. Once again Rev. K expressed her disagreement.

Following this visit, Rev. K sought out Mr. S's doctor and informed him of Mr. S's intentions. The physician immediately requested a psychiatric evaluation and further delayed Mr. S's discharge.

Aspects of the moral quandary for Rev. K

It appears that Rev. K did not keep the confidence of Mr. S. Yet clearly Rev. K acted in a way she thought was in Mr. S's best interests, seeking to protect his life. While some might find elements of paternalism here (i.e., making decisions for another without their consent, but in the belief that it is in the other's best interests), it is likely Rev. K believed she was acting with beneficent intent — that is, maximizing the good for Mr. S. From Mr. S's point-of-view, however, Rev. K may have broken the bond of confidentiality because she did not keep his secret, but rather shared it with the doctor. In this she may, indeed, have abridged Mr. S's autonomy and sought to counter his power to make autonomous decisions without interference. But I do not believe that reference to mere principles in clinical ethics is sufficient to understand the actions nor to deal with the question of confidentiality and expressed suicidal intent.

There are at least three approaches to (or models for) "doing ethics." Since, in my experience, moral conflicts are often related to model clashes, it can be helpful to understand the approach preferred by each of the participants when commenting on a particular situation.

Perhaps the best known approach to moral decision-making involves a *hierarchy of rules* which relies on overarching principles from which one deduces appropriate behaviors. A rules orientation, such as is found in many orthodox/conservative religious groups in the Western world, usually holds a few universal principles which direct moral actions. With regard to confidentiality, it is likely that only a clear and imminent threat of self-destruction would warrant a breech of secret-keeping. It is possible that Rev. K was acting in accordance with such a principled approach when she chose to share Mr. S's plans with the doctor.

Well known via the popular press, another approach to ethics is a libertarian relativism which focuses on the single principle of autonomy vis-a-vis individual situations and reduces appropriate action to what the individual seeks and wants. Most healthcare professionals believe that mental competency is necessary for truly autonomous operations. Therefore even if he agreed that Mr.

S should control his own life and death, it is not surprising that Mr. S's physician sought a psychiatric consultation.

The third overall approach is *relational*, which seeks, via induction, to negotiate virtues, principles, traditions and contexts within particular human communities of character. I would guess that both Rev. K and Mr. S are members of such a community and value some part of this approach.

One can logically and effectively argue from a rules perspective in this case, claiming, especially from some faith perspectives, that the intentional ending of a human life is never allowable, and therefore all principles must accede to this one regarding the ultimate value of life. But I believe that it is far more likely that the participants are operating from one of the other two approaches, which makes the issue of confidentiality, then, more problematic.

Some defining distinctions

The concept of confidentiality is closely related to that of secret-keeping. Indeed, both involve the drawing of boundaries to mediate the flow of information between systems. This continues to be a helpful way of thinking about confidences, but in the face of recent psychological data about the phenomenon of shame, secret-keeping can take on a more sinister cast.

Those writing about shame from both psychoanalytic and systems perspectives note that shame is related to abusive relationships and addictive patterns of behavior. Shame (from the root "skem" meaning to hide), that sense of personal flawedness, powerlessness and perpetual vulnerability to exposure, has been associated with chemical dependency, incest, and family violence. One of the ways individuals and groups seek to control the shame is to keep certain behaviors and events secret. In families organized around alcoholism, for instance, a "no talk" rule had been described as ruling operations inside and outside the family, promoting a sense of isolation.

In contrast to shame and secrecy, confidentiality (with its roots in the word for trust) is both a principle and a behavior that promotes community by drawing appropriate boundaries around persons and groups based on their inherent worth and value (as opposed to secrets which seek to mask a sense of worthlessness). A distinction is drawn, then, between *secrecy* and *confidentiality*. As used here, secrecy serves to maintain shame, while confidentiality serves to maintain trust.

A second distinction needs to be made, this one about suicide. The presence of chronic diseases, longer life expectancy, and a variety of medical technologies that can sustain the length of lives, have led many ethicists and moral theologians to consider a reformulation of the idea of suicide.

Some law-enforcement bodies define suicide in terms of "violence." Indeed many, perhaps most, suicides may be defined as violent, having to do with gunshots, hanging, carbon-monoxide poisoning, drug over-doses, etc. In each case not only is the method violent, there is also violence against the bonds of trust in the human community. When one secretly plans to end one's live for whatever reasons, leaving others to deal with the emotional ravages of the aftermath, violence is involved.

However, from time to time stories have emerged that point to suicides that were undertaken — almost always involving persons with a terminal and untreatable disease — in the context of conversations with an intimate inner circle. Some conscious and competent persons with Lou Gehrig's disease (amyotrophic lateral sclerosis), for instance, have argued for an end to their lives even though their deaths were not otherwise imminent. It may be of more than historical interest to note that as far back as the 1940s a group of leading liberal Protestant leaders petitioned the New York legislature "to permit voluntary euthanasia for incurable sufferers." While there is often a sense of something shocking about these deaths, and even moral distress, they do not encompass a quality of violence against human communities. This is precisely because they were not secrets, but rather carried-out in the context of dialogue and communal confidence. These latter events, which may be labeled as "voluntary euthanasia" or "non-violent suicide," have a fundamentally different character because of the absence of secrecy and violence. It is presumably the latter that Mr. S had in mind.

A request for confidentiality or secrecy?

In commenting on the vignette above it is important to ascertain whether Mr. S is requesting confidentiality or secrecy. While he indicates that he had talked over his decision with friends and even his mother, he has not previously engaged Rev. K in the moral conversation, though sharing his intentions with her may suggest his desire to do so. Rev. K responds to Mr. S (out of moral concern) by pointing to stories of others who have made different decisions, and she expresses her own sense of distress at his desire. What she does not do is test the confidence of Mr. S's community by asking for a meeting with his friends and mother regarding their feelings and thoughts about the decision. She could have requested Mr. S's permission to talk with these intimate relations without threatening the sense of confidentiality (as it is used here). If Mr. S were unwilling to permit such a conversation, Rev. K should suspect that his intentions are a matter of secrecy rather than confidentiality. I am arguing that in this situation *there is an obligation to keep a confidence but not a secret.*

The assessment of Mr. S's intimate community — as well as of his larger faith community — is an essential part of the medical (mental-biological), psychosocial, economic, and spiritual assessments that are required for holistic moral care. Rev. K was correct in conferring with others on the team, which is possible without breaking the bonds of confidentiality, as part of her own assessment of the situation. After all, it is only in the context of this assessment that Rev. K can answer the question: "will my action contribute to the building of trust in the moral community or will it assist in the construction of places to hide?"

Conclusion

Assuming that Rev. K was acting from a relational approach to ethics, and thus concerned to mediate and integrate established principles in the context of the stories and structures of a particular human community, it is difficult to sustain any sense that she abridged Mr. S's confidentiality. However, there are several observations that can be made about the case.

First, within the context of the faith community, Rev. K should have helped prepare members of her congregation to face issues raised by terminal and untreatable disease by addressing questions of pain and suffering as well as legal instrumentalities such as advanced directives. That Mr. S felt he could tell Rev. K of his plans suggest that he has faith in their relationship and that the community is not given to judgmental nor authoritarian behaviors. Therefore a more open dialogue about life and death decisions should have been possible.

Second, given Mr. S's intense pain and the apparent absence of any advanced directive, Rev. K was right to raise concerns about Mr. S's intentions. The principle of autonomy must be exercised in the context of competency and community.

Third, Rev. K should have been trying more to build confidence than to maintain shame in the helping relationship.

Fourth, as my colleague Russell Burck (along with some feminist ethicists) has pointed out, sometimes trust-building and trust-keeping presuppose the ability to "cover" in the service of creating and maintaining community. For instance, a beneficent concern for confidentiality around an HIV positive test result draws a protective boundary around vulnerable persons, which can mitigate the consequences of shame and stigma embedded in the larger system. Thus it serves to ensure some element of confidence between persons-in-community with an HIV positive result and the larger external community. The distinctions about secrecy and confidentiality must be carefully made so that boundaries continue to be drawn for beneficent purposes.

Finally, in all cases of which I am aware, competent persons who have expressed an interest in suicide have done so as a solution to their own profound pain and suffering and/or the fear of emotional and economic suffering for those they love. Since the focus of this chapter has been on the question of confidentiality as trust building, the final conclusion must point to the need for communities that can ensure a minimum of physical suffering, a significant degree of economic security, and sufficient meaning to maintain hopeful relationships in the midst of dying.

References

Beauchamp T, Childress J: *Principles of Biomedical Ethics.* New York, Oxford, 1979.

Bennett J: Ethical aspects of aging in America. In Clements W (editor): *Ministry With The Aging.* New York, Harper and Row, 1981.

Blumenthal S, Kupfer D (editors): *Suicide Over the Life Cycle.* Washington, DC, American Psychiatric Press, Inc., 1990.

Burton L, Grodin M: Context and process in medical ethics: The contribution of family-systems theory. *Family Systems Medicine* 6: 421-438, 1988.

Fletcher J: *Morals and Medicine.* Princeton, NJ, Princeton University Press, 1954.

Fossem M, Mason M: *Facing Shame.* New York, Norton, 1986.

Maguire D: *Death By Choice.* New York, Schocker Books, 1974.

Williams M: The right to die and the obligation to care. In Smith D, Bernstein L (editors): *No Rush To Judgment.* Bloomington, IN, Poynter Center, Indiana University, 1979.

Nathanson D: *The Many Faces of Shame.* New York, Guilford, 1987.

IV. Physical Illness and Suicide

Introduction

While ministering to persons who are sick, injured, diseased, disabled, and/or dying, it is not unusual for clergy to encounter a patient's off-hand remark that he/she "would be better off dead," or an explicit wish to die, or an explicit plan for suicide. What is the appropriate clergy response? Are suicidal wishes more understandable or less reprehensible when they arise in the context of severe physical illness or disability? In Chapter 9, Dr. Cairns discusses the problem of reconciling suicidal wishes with personal beliefs about personal autonomy, personal freedom, reverence for life, and willingness to submit to divine will. Unless the pastor has worked out his/her *personal* theology of death, dying, and suicide beforehand, it is difficult to be helpful to suicidal medical patients. Dr. Cairns also cautions that the pastor who does not agree with a sick patient's wish to die may unwittingly (by his/her choice of words) convey a message of personal rejection that fans any pre-existing suicidal crisis.

In Chapter 10, Dr. Clark questions whether public discussions of "rational suicide" and the "right-to-die" are sufficiently grounded in clinical knowledge and experience. He cites evidence that only four percent of persons who die by suicide are terminally ill, evidence that two-thirds of elderly persons who die by suicide are in relatively good physical health, and evidence that the small fraction of terminally ill persons who express suicidal wishes are generally laboring under the influence of a concomitant depressive illness.

Chapter 9

Pastoral Response to the Suicidal Medical Patient: When Is Life Truly Not Worth Living?

Nancy U. Cairns, Ph.D.

I intend to discuss three factors that seem crucial to effective ministry to the aging, the ill, and the dying. First, those who minister to these patients need some appreciation of the responses emotionally strong and healthy adults make to the psychological and social ramifications of chronic, life-threatening illness and aging. It is my belief that knowledge of the non-physical effects of chronic illness and of the ways in which people in our day and age cope with those ramifications is crucial to our ministry to ill or elderly persons contemplating suicide. The second crucial factor is the pastor's theological formulations about illness and suicide and the relationship between one's theology and one's response to the suicidal medical patient. Finally, the third essential factor is our gut response, as relatively younger and healthier individuals, to the dying or seriously debilitated parishioner. The despair and fear with which many of us confront our own eventual death can poison our ministry to those who embody our worst fears.

My ideas about this topic grew out of my work as a medical psychologist. Shortly before I completed my doctoral degree, I began work in a university medical center serving multi-handicapped retarded children and their families. After three years in that setting, I transferred to the Pediatric Oncology service, where

I spent seven years working with children with cancer and their families. During that time, I also had some contact with adult cancer patients and other adults with serious and progressive neurological disorders. One of the gifts I received from that work was an appreciation of both the horrors of life with serious illness and, more important, of the strength, courage, and creativity with which individuals and families respond to those horrors.

Since that time, in the course of my husband's seminary career and his ministry with street people in Uptown Chicago and in my own rapprochement with the Christian church, I have become increasingly aware of the power of the clergy either to help or hinder parishioners in life struggles like illness and aging. I have also been increasingly interested in the interface between clinical psychology and religious thought. Suicide, life-threatening illness, and aging accompanied by severe debility are issues that make it essential to consider that interface.

Patients' response to illness and aging

The experience of serious illness or the gradual decline in quality of life that often accompanies aging of necessity includes some degree of distress. Losses or potential losses, whether of opportunities, social contacts, abilities, or comrades and loved ones, always give rise to a grief response and to a re-appraisal and re-ordering of one's life. The accompanying feelings are often negative: numbness, shock, denial, anger, depression, or rage. For many and perhaps most of those going through such experiences, one component is some degree of suicidal thought or intention.

However, it is important to know that, for most medical patients, suicide is not the strongest, most compelling, or most attractive choice to cope with the situation, particularly after the initial shock passes. While it is true that the incidence of suicide rises gradually for adults as we age, suicide is not a common cause of adult deaths at any age. Further, although many patients with severely debilitating illness express a wish to commit suicide, and such patients have a higher risk of suicide than the general population, the percentage who attempt suicide is far from the majority. The suicide rate is highest in the 75-to 79-year-old age group, where it is 42 per 100,000 deaths (Morgan, 1989, p. 240). Older white males have the highest risk of suicide. However, death by suicide is far less common than death from other causes (heart disease, cancer, or cerebrovascular disease, for example) in this age group.

One implication of the demographics of suicide is that *suicide is by no means an inevitable or even a common response to illness, aging, or the threat of death.* A careful assessment of those elderly or seriously ill people who do attempt to commit suicide will most often show that there are other factors that make suicide appear to be the only option worth taking at the time. These factors may include lack of social support, lack of financial support, a sense of helplessness and hopelessness, or a loss of the ability to do what one sees as crucial to being oneself. Often, there are also significant precipitating events that "the patient interprets as rejection from family and physician" (Shneidman, Farberow, & Litman, 1983, p. 263) and, I would add, from the minister. The suicidal medical patient is responding to these kinds of stresses, not illness or aging *per se*. It may well be possible to help a person recover from or cope with these events, with the result that she/he is no longer suicidal. In the words of Edwin Shneidman (1985, p. 124), "... the main clinical rule is: Reduce the level of suffering, often just a little bit, and the individual will choose to live."

In seven years of working with children with cancer, about half of whom eventually died of the disease, I often heard children and adolescents say "I hate this. I don't want any more treatment. It's not worth it; I'd rather just die." However, there was one group of patients who never voiced such thoughts: those whose parents would have *allowed* them to discontinue treatment and die. When given a chance to talk in private about their wishes, children whose parents were themselves despairing and willing to give up the struggle universally chose to continue their treatment and continue to live. Although they were just as angry, just as distressed, and in just as much pain as others who voiced a wish to die, they avoided doing so. I think it was because they knew they might be taken up on the offer, and they did not want to die. I have had less experience with adult patients, but the experience has been similar. Talk of or gestures toward suicide are a way of saying, "I can't stand life the way it is; recognize that, be with me, and help me to change it." If we provide that help, patients almost always choose life.

The implication of the rarity of true suicidal intent among medical patients is that it is crucial to allow a parishioner adequate time and space to explore and express her or his true feelings, wishes, and intentions. It is only through intense dialogue that we and our parishioners can be clear about what they are really saying and what they are really asking from us.

There are many ways in which we can be with people and help to reduce their suffering "often just a little bit." In addition to being there and listening in a deeply attentive way, we can often take concrete steps to make life easier. One is as advocates or ombudsmen for parishioners who are medical patients. In the high-tech, highly specialized modern hospital, with its shortages of nurses and other non-physician personnel, there is often no one who considers the welfare of the patient as a whole person. The oncologists looks at the tumor, the radiologist looks at total radiation exposure, the nephrologist looks at liver function, the renologist at kidney function, and so on. Among all these specialists, there may be no one who notices that the patient has had increasingly inadequate pain control for the past six weeks or that friends who were very attentive at first have "run out of steam" during the years of the patient's struggle with illness. The minister or chaplain can pay attention to the whole person and act as intermediary with the medical staff. Clergy are not in a position to have a direct influence on physical well-being. We can, however, make sure that direct caregivers know about problems that, if left untreated, will increase a person's despair and therefore increase suicide risk.

Another practical way to help is to attend to parishioners during periods when other supports have been withdrawn. For example, for a chronically ill person, leaving the hospital may feel like abandonment. Although hospitals are seldom as emotionally supportive as we would like, they nonetheless provide care and the companionship of other patients as well as hospital staff. The person who is discharged to the apartment in which she/he lives alone often confronts not only increasing physical limitations but also loneliness and isolation. This period may be the time of greatest risk, given the combination of withdrawal of social support, the physical and mental ability to execute a suicide plan, and the expectation of deterioration and a lonely, painful, or shameful death. Again, it is important to remember that people respond well to very slight reductions in suffering. The minister's ability and willingness to maintain social contact and mobilize other parishioners to keep in touch with visits, phone calls, or letters can make all the difference in whether life is experienced as worthwhile.

Personal theological formulation about suicide

Suicide is not simply a psychological, psychiatric, emotional, or social issue. It is also a theological issue. It is important that, before encountering a parishioner who is contemplating suicide or requesting assistance in dying, the minister have her/his personal theology clearly in mind. Although formulating a personal theology around this issue may not be possible in the abstract, it is important at least to begin before one is in a situation that demands a pastoral response. One reason is that, in a crisis, few of us think clearly. And an interaction with a desperately ill and suicidal parishioner is certainly a crisis.

Another reason is that, going back to what we know about sick people who seriously consider suicide, one precipitating factor can be perception of rejection by others. Unless our theological views are well thought out and encompass ideas of compassion as well as sin, we can all too easily precipitate a suicide by tapping into and intensifying the patient's sense of hopelessness, helplessness, worthlessness, isolation, and shame. If our theology does not allow us the freedom and comfort to sit with the patient in a ministry of presence and accept the reality of her/his suffering, we risk being part of the rejection that so often intensifies suicidal thought and intent.

Any member of the clergy might be said to have a personal theology of death and, within that broad category, personal theologies of suicide and euthanasia. This personal theology is in part a reflection of the teachings of one's religious tradition. The Judaeo-Christian tradition, like Buddhism, Islam, and the other great religions of the world, has a great deal to say about suicide and passive or active euthanasia. However, our tradition is not monolithic in its views.

The prohibition against suicide has not always existed in the Christian Church. Neither the Hebrew nor the Christian Bible explicitly prohibits suicide. Christian ideas about suicide, which to a great extent are Western ideas about suicide, date from approximately the fourth century. These ideas were first promulgated by St. Augustine:

> ... for essentially non-religious reasons. Historically, the excessive martyrdom of early Christians frightened the church elders sufficiently for them to seek to introduce a serious deterrent. Augustine did this by relating suicide to sin. We now know that Augustine was not against suicide on chiefly theological grounds. He was primarily against the decimation of Christians by suicide and, even more narrowly, against the suicide by Christians only for reasons of martyrdom... Suicide by reason of physical or emotional suffering, old age, altruism toward others, personal honor, illness, and the like — in short, the very reasons with which 99.9% of the suicides committed nowadays are associated — were not the target of Augustine's writings. (Battin, 1982, quoted in Shneidman, 1988, pp. 30-31).

Whether or not a prohibition against suicide existed in early Christian or Jewish theology, there is little doubt than most current Judaeo-Christian thinking prohibits suicide. For example, the view that suicide is not justifiable on theological grounds predominates among the theologians contributing to this volume. These contributors agree that life is a gift of God and that one's highest calling is to respect and cherish that gift until God chooses to withdraw it. A choice to end one's own life is then a usurpation of divine authority and an expression of profound ingratitude. Each minister, priest, or rabbi, as an individual, can draw on this predominant strain of thought.

Against this theological position some weigh the value many westerners attach to autonomy and to individual freedom and responsibility. These values lead some to conclude that there is a right to choose a way of death as well as a way of life. When life becomes insupportable, when life has no positive quality, one might well have the right to end it.

The personal theology of any particular member of the clergy will be shaped, at minimum, by these two opposing theological ideas as well as by personal experiences and attitudes. In balancing autonomy against a reverence for life and/or a willingness to submit to the divine will, many will judge that the latter values weigh more heavily. However, in communicating that judgment to a suicidal parishioner, one must be very careful not to imply rejection. In rejecting the choice, one must not reject the person who chooses.

It is equally important to be careful in communicating the notion that suicide might be theologically justifiable and psychologically rational. In agreeing that the parishioner's life may not be worth living, and that therefore suicide may be justified, the minister can unwittingly convey rejection. At a deep and intensely personal level, permission to commit suicide can mean that even the minister is abandoning the sick person.

Personal responses to the dying

I have considered the minister's theological response to the suicidal patient. It is at least as important to think about our personal response to illness, disability, and death as it is to think about our theological response. This is a topic about which it is virtually impossible to be neutral, for the simple reason that in contemplating another's vulnerability and approaching death, we necessarily confront our own. The response to that confrontation can, in the absence of efforts to resolve these issues, make it difficult if not impossible to enter into the other person's world as we must if we are to be truly helpful.

The importance of this kind of self-scrutiny stems from a sense that, to a great extent, our ideas about suicide or euthanasia for patients who are "hopeless" arise from our own despair about illness, aging, disability, and death. We see ourselves in the patient who has lost control of bodily functions, has lost loved ones, employment, comfort, and, we assume, hope. The immediate response is, "I would not want to live this way." It is that response that can blind us to the true state and needs of the patient. My own experience is that I am often very distressed by the suffering that others endure. I see people in pain, isolated, unable to care for themselves, and I can see little joy or even comfort in their lives. In the face of this kind of suffering, I have often wished for a quick and painless release. However, it does not follow that the patient also wishes for death. Those who think to ask will often learn that the patient can find meaning and even pleasure in a life that looks hopeless to an observer. The fact is, I have been suicidal *on behalf of my patients* far more often than my patients have been suicidal on behalf of themselves.

In working with desperately ill people, I have become convinced that, when I actually experience this kind of pain, I will want to live through it, particularly if I can be assured of doing so in any kind of community. I very much hope that at that point, my pastor will be able to be with me because she/he will have made peace, or at least declared a truce, with suffering and death in a meaningful personal way. If we have not reached such a position of peace and acceptance, we must at least be able to recognize our own struggle with the idea of death and helplessness and, having recognized it, be able to set it aside so that it need not get in the way of hearing either a parishioner's suffering or a parishioner's joy. While there may be concrete steps we can take to reduce that person's suffering "just a little bit," those steps are usually less important than the first giant step of simply being with the sufferer, recognizing the suffering, and validating the worth of the life lived in suffering.

References

Battin MP: *Ethical Issues in Suicide.* Englewood Cliffs, NJ, Prentice-Hall, 1982.

Morgan AC: Special issues of assessment and treatment of suicide risk in the elderly. In Jacobs D, Brown HN (editors): *Suicide: Understanding and Responding. Harvard Medical School Perspectives.* Madison, CT, International Universities Press, 1989, pages 239-255.

Shneidman E: *Definition of Suicide.* New York, John Wiley & Sons, 1985.

Shneidman ES, Farberow NL, Litman RE: *The Psychology of Suicide.* New York, Jason Aronson, 1983.

Chapter 10

Are Wishes to Implement a "Rational Suicide" Usually Justified and Usually Rational?

David C. Clark, Ph.D.

A number of different groups advocate laws permitting persons with a terminal illness and those experiencing unrelieved pain to end their own lives with few or no obstacles, and laws permitting physicians to help the same persons die. As a faculty member at a metropolitan teaching hospital and a psychologist who specializes in treating mood disorders and suicidal behavior, I find that the accompanying public debate about "rational suicide" and physician-assisted suicide is consistently and dangerously oversimplified.

It is a serious mistake to believe that the suicidal communications of the ill should *always* be accepted at face value, without considering the possibility that a person talking about suicide may harbor several different wishes that need to be understood in their entirety before any reasonable conclusions can be reached about what the person really wants. Second, psychiatric illness plays a pivotal role in the genesis of suicidal despair, but this fact is rarely highlighted in discussions of "rational suicide." Third, research and clinical experience in medical and hospice settings consistently shows that only a small proportion of medically ill patients express suicidal wishes, and then not necessarily the ones in greater pain or those dying. Fourth, it is important to consider potential social effects of a legalized "right to die" on younger persons — particularly adolescents — at risk for death by suicide.

Any thoughtful and informed discussion about "rational suicide" and the "right-to-die" should include the following information.

(1) Suicide is a major public health problem. Suicide is the eighth leading cause of death in the United States, accounting for more than 30,000 deaths each year. When the leading causes of death are ranked according to "years of life lost prior to age 65," suicide rises to become the fourth leading cause of death. Thus it should be clear that suicide is not a rare problem and not a narrowly-defined mental health problem — it is a widespread public health problem.

(2) Old age and suicide are not parallel or inextricably interwoven processes. Sixty years ago, the suicide rate for the elderly portion of the U.S. population was three times higher than it is now. The elderly suicide rate has declined steadily since that time, reaching a low point for this century in 1981, rising slightly between 1981 and 1987, and declining again since.

Although elderly white males die by suicide at a rate higher than that for any other age group, the same is not true for females, blacks, or Hispanics. For women, the risk of suicide is greatest in middle age, and declines after age 65. For blacks and Hispanics, the risk of suicide is greatest in young adulthood.

(3) The vast majority of persons who die by suicide are in good physical health in the weeks and months preceding their death. Community-based studies of suicides in the United States, England, Sweden, Australia, and other countries consistently agree on the fact that no more than two to six percent of all persons who die by suicide were terminally ill. In one of the first community-based studies of suicide by persons aged 65 years and over, two-thirds of the older adults were in relatively good physical health when they died by suicide according to autopsy findings, medical records, and face-to-face interviews with the next-of-kin.

(4) At least 93% of persons who die by suicide evidence symptoms of major psychiatric illness in the weeks before death — usually depressive illness or alcoholism. While the psychiatric symptoms can be documented by interviews with family members and friends after the suicide, more than half of all suicide victims had never seen a mental health professional in their lifetime, and more than half had never made a suicide attempt before. Thus the symptoms of psychiatric illness that are so common among suicide victims were generally not recognized by the suicide victim or the victim's family members beforehand.

(5) **Depressive illness is a** *temporary* **and** *treatable* **condition that frequently goes unrecognized, untreated, or inadequately treated.** Symptoms common to depressive illness include: pervasive sadness, apathy, irritability, trouble sleeping, appetite and/or weight changes, preoccupation with death or suicide, loss of interest in activities that until recently were considered fun, hopelessness, and loss of insight. Depressed persons are often the last to recognize the severity of their own symptoms, often deny that they are ill when questioned, and often resist accepting help from others. Only a third of all persons suffering under the yoke of a depressive illness ever seek treatment, despite evidence that more than two-thirds of all depressed patients respond well to brief psychotherapies, antidepressant medications, and/or a combination of the two.

(6) **Depressed persons tend to become** *preoccupied* **with their physical symptoms and physical health.** Sometimes their physical preoccupations and despair combine to make them *erroneously* believe they are dying (for example, of cancer), even after medical evidence and their doctors have conclusively contradicted their belief. Many who erroneously believe they are dying avoid further contact with physicians, preferring to be "left alone to die." In two community-based studies of elderly persons who died by suicide, there were more persons who killed themselves because they *mistakenly* believed they had cancer than there were persons who died ill with cancer or any other terminal illness.

(7) **Most terminally or severely ill patients who express suicidal intentions are laboring under the influence of a transient and treatable psychiatric illness — once again, usually depressive illness.** This can be made apparent by undertaking interviews with close family members and close friends, or by observing the patient closely over time. One generally observes that suicide intent waxes and wanes over time. Terminally ill patients who voice suicidal thoughts generally respond well to standard treatments for depressive illness — psychotherapy and antide-

pressant medication. Patients in pain generally respond well to good medical pain management measures. After a brief course of treatment for depressive illness, both groups of patients are usually grateful that no one facilitated the suicide they were planning while they were *temporarily* depressed or in pain.

(8) **Medical professionals working with terminally ill patients consistently find that the overwhelming majority cling to life throughout their illness.** While many assume that persons with chronic, painful, or terminal illnesses opt to end their suffering prematurely by opting for suicide, in fact this type of choice — usually referred to as "rational" suicide — is seen rarely in hospital and hospice work. Except in those cases where physical illness is accompanied by a major depressive illness, the great majority of patients spontaneously reject the suicide option and choose to die naturally. The majority of terminally ill patients cling to life throughout their illnesses. Among elderly persons, for whom chronic painful illnesses are not uncommon, only 0.5% of male deaths and 0.2% of female deaths are attributable to suicide.

(9) **The question of mental competence to opt for suicide.** Attention to the impact of acute psychiatric illness on rational decision-making has been missing from serious discussions of "rational" suicide. Most ethicists and caregivers agree that ethical decisions about assisted suicide, for example, require that the subject's judgment not be compromised by mental disorders such as depressive illness. Advocates of "rational" suicide offer many case examples of persons who chose suicide or assisted suicide in a "rational" state of mind, but of course most of the individuals in question were never evaluated by an experienced mental health professional. The facts that the subject had never seen a mental health professional in his/her life, or that he/she had been a healthy and productive citizen for most of his/her life, do not constitute convincing evidence of the absence of acute psychopathology at the time of death.

In the absence of consensual clinical standards for assessing "rationality" or "mental competence," the determination is extremely susceptible to personal biases about aging, old age, and the psychological effects of chronic disease. "Ageism," or "a physician's under-estimation of the remediable nature of depressive illness in an elderly patient, the decision to take a less aggressive approach to pain management in a patient with cancer, or the validation of a patient's suicidal thoughts when unrecognized alternatives exist" (Richardson and colleagues, 1989), has the potential to express itself and influence care delivery insidiously when evaluating competence — in the form of a belief that it is *futile* to treat the psychological or physical afflictions of the elderly. The argument goes: "They have already lived the better part of their lives. They are already so near to death anyway." All too often, subtle degrees of "ageism" distort our understanding of why a specific instance of suicide has occurred, and tempt us to misunderstand the case as an example of "rational suicide" or a psychologically sound person's "right to die." While we do not preclude the possibility of "rational suicide," we suspect that there is a strong cultural bias to overlook the psychiatric forces and motives implicated in cases of elderly suicide.

(10) **The problem of social imitation.** Imagine the situation of a nineteen-year-old boy who is anguished and desperate after breaking up with a girlfriend of two years. Because the adolescent cannot imagine ever finding another love to equal the one he just lost, he begins to contemplate his own death. In the back of his mind he remembers that his grandfather made a sanctioned decision to end his own life some months earlier. The grandfather chose to die because his life quality slipped below the minimal level he was prepared to tolerate — he was in pain and his physical functioning was compromised. Who is to explain to the adolescent that the two situations are not comparable? In the classroom, some adolescents possess the intellect and maturity to understand that most discussions of "rational suicide" are confined to examples of persons likely to die in the space of the next six months — the usual definition of "terminal illness." But when their own life is in upheaval, even bright and mature adolescents do not always grasp these kinds of distinctions.

Conclusion

The wish to end life by killing oneself is almost always a serious symptom arising from a temporary psychiatric illness. While the subtlety and complexity of depressive illnesses often make it difficult for loved ones to recognize the gravity of the problem, it is generally a mistake to assume that a wish to die or to end one's own life is a rational, carefully thought-through decision justified by a person's life situation or health status. One should always suspect that an unrecognized psychiatric illness has silently, invisibly influenced the judgment of a patient opting for suicide. Depressive and other psychiatric illnesses often rob medically ill patients of hope and objectivity, comprising their ability to exercise any well-considered "right-to-die" decision. Compromised intellect, compromised judgment, and loss of insight are usually transient symptoms, extensions of the prevailing depressive illness, but they are hard to document outside of the context of a psychiatric evaluation. When a patient asks to die, the burden of proof should lie on the shoulders of those who wish to defend the wish as a rational decision.

References

Brown JH, Henteleff P, Barakat S, Rowe CJ: Is it normal for terminally ill patients to desire death? *American Journal of Psychiatry* 143: 208-211, 1986.

Clark DC: "Rational" suicide and people with terminal conditions or disabilities. *Issues in Law and Medicine* 8: 147-166, 1992.

Clark DC: *Elderly Suicide: Final report submitted to the Andrus Foundation.* Washington, DC, American Association of Retired Persons, 1991.

Conwell Y, Caine ED, Olsen K: Suicide and cancer in late life. *Hospital and Community Psychiatry* 41: 1334-1339, 1990.

Conwell Y, Caine ED: Sounding Board: Rational suicide and the right to die — Reality and myth. *New England Journal of Medicine* 325: 1100-1102, 1991.

Conwell Y, Rotenberg M, Caine ED: Completed suicide at age 50 and over. *Journal of the American Geriatrics Society* 38: 640-644, 1990.

Lee MA: Depression and refusal of life support in older people: An ethical dilemma. *Journal of the American Geriatrics Society* 38: 710-714, 1990.

Murphy GK: Cancer and the coroner. *Journal of the American Medical Association* 237: 786-788, 1977.

Richardson R, Lowenstein S, Weissberg M: Coping with the suicidal elderly: A physician's guide. *Geriatrics* 44: 43-51, 1989.

V. Grief After Suicide

Introduction

The experience of losing a family member by suicide is beyond words. In Chapter 11, Rev. Hinrichs graciously shares the experience of losing his 14-year-old daughter Susan by suicide, and summarizes what the experience has taught him about grief after suicide. Rev. Hinrichs' eloquent account helps the reader fathom the world of those bereaved by suicide, helps us consider the unique problem posed by the high visibility of the pastor's family when that family experiences a suicide, and helps us understand that it could happen to any of us.

The next two chapters describe two clergymen's wealth of experience providing pastoral care to those bereaved by suicide. In Chapter 12, Rabbi Marx describes his sense of how the cleric can work to close the gulf between "a sense of the holy" and the pain of loss by suicide. In Chapter 13, Father Rubey discusses the meaningfulness of funerals, rituals, and anniversaries for suicide survivors, and shares his belief that a death by suicide should be interpreted in terms of its medical rather than its moral implications for the benefit of surviving family members.

Chapter 11

Surviving and Healing After a Suicide: A Pastoral Perspective

Rev. Eimo E. Hinrichs, M.Div., S.T.M.

On December 14, 1984, the life of our beautiful 14-year-old adoptive daughter, Susan, suddenly came to an end as a result of an overdose of my wife's prescription medication. I immediately found myself overwhelmed with the tumultuous emotions that countless others have experienced because of this tragic form of death. In the journey that led me to a search for healing and a sense of meaning to my life, I came into contact with many others who have suffered as I have. Ultimately, this led to the formation of a Survivors of Suicide support group in 1989. My wife and I serve as co-facilitators of this group.

Although each person's experience of grief is unique, and although each person grieves in his or her own individual way, there seem to be universal feelings and emotions that throw the world of a survivor into chaos. Much of what I have to say will be intensely personal; at the same time, my remarks will incorporate what other survivors have shared. The latter have confirmed that much of that which we experience is quite similar.

Modern-day stigma and ostracism

In the Middle Ages, European law required the forfeiture of all a family's money and property to the state as punishment for a suicide (interestingly, the word *coroner* has its origins in the function of deciding which deaths were suicides, where the verdict of suicide meant that all assets were forfeit to the crown). Thus most familial survivors had economic as well as psychological reasons for maintaining that the cause of death was not suicide. In recent centuries, the law has allowed survivors to keep their inheritances, but suicide has increasingly come to be viewed as evidence of *familial* as well as personal failure. A societal judgment prevails against the family, implying that they somehow caused or contributed to the suicidal death. The potential for shame, stigma, and loss of face often leads to suicide being guarded as a dark family secret, to be kept underground at all costs (Colt, 1987; Buechner, 1991). Thus familial survivors often continue to conceal a suicidal death by a variety of means, as was true in the Middle Ages.

Survivors today still have an uneasy feeling they have something to hide. They struggle to rid themselves of centuries of accumulated stigma. While society still tends to stigmatize and ostracize survivors, the punishments today are largely emotional and psychological (Colt, 1987). For example, if a teenager dies by suicide, society generally assumes it was because of a disturbed family situation and that the parents particularly are at fault. The surviving spouse of a suicide victim is often blamed for having created a bad marital situation.

How many familial survivors of suicide are there? There are approximately 30,000 recorded suicides each year in the United States. If we assume there is an average of six survivors in each immediate family, then there are 180,000 new survivors annually, or 1,800,000 each decade. If one counts extended family members and close friends directly affected by the suicide, the number of survivors easily quadruples. Every congregation will have someone who has been affected in a personal way by suicide.

Shock, disbelief, denial

As would be true for any sudden, traumatic death, there are first of all the initial feelings of shock, disbelief, and denial.

Having a loved one die in this way is so incredible, our inner being can face up to the reality of what actually happened only gradually. For weeks, I found myself looking in my daughter's bedroom in the morning, expecting that she had come back during the night. When school let out for the day, my wife found herself watching for her to come down the street along with all the other teenagers.

It seemed like we were often walking around in a fog. We were just going through the motions of a daily routine and none of it made much sense. Oftentimes, we felt like we were having a bad dream and that if we woke up from it, we would find that none of this really happened. Occasionally, some people can remain stuck at this point in their grief for months or even for years, basically denying the reality of what happened.

The crazy period

Once the shock and feelings of numbness begin to wear off, the full impact of the tragedy begins to be felt. A common reaction people have to their feelings of intense grief is, "I must be going crazy." Normal thoughts and behaviors that are experienced in intense grief are totally different from what one normally experiences. The grieving person does not know whether what is being experienced is normal or abnormal.

During this so-called crazy period, there may be periods of confusion and disorganization, along with memory lapses. There are frequently difficulties in eating and a universal disruption of sleeping patterns. There may be visual and auditory hallucinations involving the deceased. Dr. Alan Wolfelt, a nationally known thanatologist, states that visual hallucinations are so common amongst grieving people that he prefers to call them "memory pictures" instead (Wolfelt, 1988). These memory pictures are a part of the searching and yearning process the mourner goes through in desiring the presence of the deceased. There may also be disturbing dreams about the dead person. These dreams can be considered as an unconscious means of search for the loved one who has died.

Shame and stigma

Along with the usual emotions grievers experience, survivors of suicide live with intense feelings of shame and stigma. When I walked through a grocery store, it felt like I was wearing a sign that said, "My daughter killed herself." Wherever I went, I had the irrational, uneasy feeling that people somehow knew. I believed that those who knew thought of me as a bad person. There were a few times people actually avoided meeting us in a store. In retrospect, they probably could not deal with what happened or didn't know what to say to us. But, at the time, we felt shunned by them.

When our local newspaper published an article of my daughter's death with a bold headline on the back page of both the Friday evening and Saturday morning editions, I felt like my shame had been exposed to the entire world. I also felt exploited and used by the news media for the purpose of sensationalism. When I saw the repeat article in the Saturday edition, I was so angry I furiously threw the paper to the floor and let fly with some unministerial expletives!

This sense of shame, of being stigmatized, causes some survivors to withdraw and isolate themselves. Some never get to the point where they can share their feelings with anyone else because of the fear of experiencing further shame, hurt, and pain. Initially, some find it hard even to open up with a group of fellow survivors.

Grief progression

Mental health professionals sometimes mistakenly label normal expressions of grief by survivors as pathological because the expressions so often appear "too intense" to those unfamiliar with grief after suicide. What can be expected in the normal grief process of a survivor?

As is true in any death, there are definite stages of grief. But don't look for a neatly defined five stages of grief as delineated by Elizabeth Kubler-Ross. There have been sad stories of counselors who felt their main task with grieving people was to move them from one prefabricated stage to another. This results in an overly clinical, overly academic approach to the griever, who ends up feeling rejected, misunderstood, and isolated.

There were times when my emotions were so volatile that anyone could have detected all the stages of grief, except for acceptance, in a particular day. Even at the point of this writing, some seven years after my daughter's death, there are still times when I experience intense pain and sadness. Fortunately, the intensity and the duration of the pain is not nearly as great as it was several years ago. I am convinced that there will always be remnants of grief. Contrary to popular belief, it is not something that one gets over after a few months or a few years. Rather, it is something to be integrated and worked through so that it is possible to go on with life. At the same time, I will never be the same person I was before. I see myself as having become a "wounded healer," so that the healing I have experienced for my wounds makes it possible to reach out to others as an instrument of God's healing power (Nouwen, 1972).

Guilt

Guilt appears to be a universal emotion of survivors. There is no kind of death that seems so successful in laying a guilt trip as does a suicide. Even people who did not know the person well often feel some of this. They, too, will experience a sense of responsibility revolving around the many "if onlies:" If only I had not said or would have said this or that; If only I had done or not done this or that, etc., then she/he would not have committed suicide. For parents, there are overwhelming feelings of: Where did I go wrong? Where did I fail as a parent? Why didn't I notice the signs and symptoms?

For myself, there was an added burden of guilt. I have been professionally trained to recognize the signs and symptoms of suicidal thinking and behavior. Yet I failed to detect them in my own daughter. Also, I was the only one home with her at the time she was taking her overdose.

There is no quick way through this guilt. This was one of the painful realizations that led my wife and me to seek out help by going to a grief support group offered by one of our local hospitals. We felt like we were wearing out our friends by always feeling the need to talk about Susan's death. And this is what gave us a sense of relief to be in a support group — that here we could say anything we were thinking or feeling and others would understand what we were going through.

With regard to the guilt, we heard Iris Bolton, the author of *My Son, My Son* (Bolton, 1983) address a group of survivors to the effect that we have to keep talking about how we are guilty until we wear it out and can let go of it. And this is also what we experienced. As pastors, we need to be careful not to shut off a survivor by saying, "You don't need to feel guilty anymore; you did the best you could." (Eventually, there will be a proper time to say this as a way of giving reassurance). The most important thing is to keep listening, to allow the person to talk, and for the listener to reflect on what a painful burden this guilt must be. Allow the survivor to own his or her feelings instead of implying how she/he should be feeling.

With regard to the availability of God's forgiveness for the guilt-ridden person, I believe God's love is present simply in another person listening and accepting. God, too, is suffering along with the guilt-ridden person. A person needs to go through a feeling before being able to get beyond it. This journey can be facilitated by the caring presence of an understanding listener as a manifestation of God's caring and love.

Anger

Anger is another universal emotion of survivors. The anger may go in many different directions. At some point or another, it will be directed toward the deceased. The anger may arise because of all the pain caused by the death. There may be feelings of having been rejected and abandoned by the deceased. There may be anger toward the deceased for not having accepted help. On the unconscious level, the person who commits suicide might have been lashing out in a hostile way at those around her/him. We need to recognize, however, that most who die by suicide are not thinking about all the hurt survivors will experience. I have talked to a number of persons who have survived a serious attempt, and they generally say the main thing they were thinking about during the attempt was how to get rid of inner pain that felt unbearable and overwhelming.

Anger might be felt toward other people who appear to be insensitive to the pain the mourner is experiencing. Or the grieving person might feel angry simply because everyone else seems to be enjoying life whereas she/he is hurting so much.

There will often be anger toward people in the medical field who failed to save the life of the deceased. Many survivors feel anger toward mental health professionals who seemingly botched things up in their treatment efforts or who failed to intervene at a critical moment. Some might feel anger toward police involved at the death scene who appeared callused, indifferent, or even hostile.

Some of the anger I felt was directed toward myself because I felt I had failed to be the kind of father I should have been for my daughter. Even though we were aware our daughter had emotional problems and she was getting professional counseling, my wife and I had hoped that our love for her and God's love for her would eventually enable her to turn her life around.

I also felt anger toward society in general because of the kind of world in which teenagers are required to live. I was angry at some of my daughter's peers and the various forms of peer pressure that had destructive influences on her.

Anger at clergy and anger at God

Clergy often become targets of the anger and hostility of mourners. The basic anger is probably being felt toward God. Since He often seems remote and far away, a visible clergyperson easily becomes a substitute target. Some people find it difficult to acknowledge that they are angry with God. There seems to be a fear of divine retribution if one openly speaks to God about being angry with him. At the least, many have the feeling it's not quite safe or acceptable to bring this feeling into the open.

I have oftentimes pointed people to the Psalms as a way of helping them acknowledge and express their anger to God. It can be a relief to discover that the psalmists were able to lash out at God in the context of prayer, and that He listened and accepted what they communicated. There were times when it seemed like anger was the only emotion being expressed in my prayers. Fortunately, I experienced that God had big enough shoulders to handle it. I also discovered that with God, as with anyone else, it's hard to talk to a person when you're mad at them. Deep down, I knew that God was not the cause of what had gone wrong. But sometimes, it seemed like no one else could be blamed. When one can experience that God's love is great enough to accept even the strongest negative feelings, it can be a great relief to verbalize those feelings to Him.

Guilt and anger are the hardest emotions with which to deal in our culture. A person needs to have permission to mourn — to feel the full intensity of these emotions. Assurance needs to be given that it's okay to get mad, even at God.

Fear

Irrational fear is another common emotion of survivors. Perhaps because of the extremely traumatic nature of a suicidal death, many survivors experience a nameless kind of fear — a feeling like nothing is certain or secure. It's like the whole experience has to be relived over and over again until the inner self can finally cope with the terror and horror of what happened. This is one reason why survivors feel the need to simply tell the story of what happened over and over again. Don't assume that having a few sessions with a person, where the story is told with the full intensity of emotion, will resolve that need.

Survivors often have fears that something will happen to one of their other surviving children or other family members. If something so tragic happened to the one who died, what could prevent something equally tragic happening to another family member?

The anxiety level of surviving parents can shoot up quickly if one of their teenagers is a half hour late coming home. Or, if a teenager is exhibiting a lot of moodiness and is frequently withdrawing and isolating her/himself, there might be fear that this child could also make a suicide attempt.

I did not have the fear that one of our surviving children would attempt suicide. But I did have anxieties about some other tragic event overtaking them. I had fears that my wife might become sick and that she too could die. I also had irrational fears about my own physical health and well-being. I was aware that grief can affect physical as well as emotional health. At times, I was obsessed with the possibility that I might develop high blood pressure or other stress-related illnesses.

I also had fears about my sanity — that I might lose it and go off the deep end. A depression that hung on for a number of months distorted my ability to feel hopeful about the future. Some survivors become suicidal as a result of their deep depression. In addition to the suicidal thoughts commonly fostered by depression, the option of suicide might also appear attractive because it would reunite the survivor with the deceased. Even small children make statements of wishing to die in order to be with the deceased parent.

There were also fears and doubts about my ability to be effective on a professional level. Because of a lower energy level, I became fatigued more easily. I was less efficient because of inabilities to concentrate and focus on things that needed doing. There was also a feeling of being a failure, professionally speaking, because I had failed to prevent the death of my daughter.

Search for a reason

Another common phenomenon in the grief process is that survivors tend to search for the reason why the suicidal death occurred. Every survivor attempts to piece together various reasons for why the person chose to end her/his life. For a small number of survivors, their grief becomes pathological in the sense that they remain in a state of denial. They keep maintaining the death was an accident or even try to explain that someone else murdered the deceased. For some, it is not until many years later that they are able to let go of their denial. Some never do.

There is never a single-cause explanation for a suicidal death. It is always complex and multi-faceted. But even though a number of factors seem to fit together that would explain the death, the real reasons are hidden within the person who died. There's usually a certain amount of mystery as to why it happened and particularly why it took place at a certain time.

The main reason why the majority of suicidal deaths occur is because of a major depression. Oftentimes, the depression had never been diagnosed or treated. It would appear that the person who died was primarily trying to get rid of overwhelming inner psychic pain. At the particular time the attempt was made, there seemed to be no hope the pain would ever go away. The desire to get rid of pain is perhaps more prominent than the wish to die. It is only after surviving a suicide attempt that many attempters realize how much it would have hurt other people. A deep major depression can constrict one's emotional awareness of the feelings of others so much that one is focused only on one's own overwhelming inner pain.

A mourner needs to keep asking the question of why the person died over and over. The survivor needs to wear it out so that she/he can finally let go of it. Probably, the question never goes away completely for most of us survivors. But hopefully a time will come when it's not quite as important to have an answer for what appears to be an unanswerable question. Never fully knowing why the person died is another way of experiencing feelings of helplessness and powerlessness. For those who have a meaningful religious faith, there is the hope that eventually they will experience the most important answer to their many anguished questions: the fact that God's love and mercy will never abandon us.

Desire for meaning

Along with the feeling that the suicidal death is meaningless, senseless, and irrational, there's also a feeling survivors have that something good needs to come out of this experience, or else it will continue to be senseless, meaningless, and irrational. Right at the beginning, my wife and I wanted something positive to come out of this experience so that we could be used to reach out to other hurting people, especially teenagers. One of the ways this has happened is through the formation of the Survivors of Suicide support group. There have been opportunities to speak to teenagers, professional groups, and other community groups on the subject of teenage suicide, grief after suicide, etc.

Other survivors have also experienced that their lives can still be meaningful as they reach out and become concerned about the needs and hurts of others. There is often a heightened sensitivity to the suffering of others, which enables God to use recovering survivors as wounded healers.

Acceptance

Elizabeth Kubler-Ross delineates acceptance as the last state in the grief process. If by acceptance one means you never feel any more pain over the death, I doubt if anyone ever achieves this stage. Even seven years after our daughter's death, there are still memories which can be stirred up which result in moments of sharp, intense pain and grief. But the pain is no longer as prolonged or as intense as it once was. Generally, I can believe that life is hopeful and meaningful. I am able to have a feeling of gratitude that we were privileged to have Susan come into our family when she was nine months old, and that we have some happy memories of her growth and development. At the same time, there is a sadness that life with so much potential was wasted by ending so prematurely.

As stated before, many people in our society assume that after a few months, one should be pretty well over a grief experience. Dr. Alan Wolfelt, in a presentation he made to a group of clergy in Peoria, stated it takes at least three-and-one-half to four years on average to work through the various tasks of mourning. However, there is no specific time frame that can be established for an individual. Each person has her/his own unique way of working through the grief and integrating it into the ongoing process of life.

On the other hand, there are those who will comment to survivors: "You'll never get over this." It is true that in a sense one never "gets over" it. I am convinced that there will always be fragments of grief that will stir up from time to time throughout my life. But in spite of that, I can also affirm that one can survive. There is healing which can take place to the point that one can continue to cope with life in a positive and constructive way. As clergy, we have unique opportunities to be used as instruments of God's healing. We have the ability to sensitize other people to the needs of those who are grieving and to enable a community of faith to offer caring, supportive relationships to those who are hurting.

There are particular times when we need to give special attention to survivors, such as the anniversary of the death and during the major holidays, especially during the first year of grief. We as clergy can invite survivors to get together with us from time to time simply to talk, while we offer a sensitive ear to listen. We can mobilize other caring people to surround them with supportive, loving relationships. Also, we can encourage them to participate in a grief support group, if one is available in the community. However, not everyone feels comfortable participating in a group experience.

The scriptures urge us to "weep with those who weep." Too often in the past, survivors of suicide have had to weep in isolation, feeling overwhelmed with a feeling of societal stigma. We as clergy can take the leadership in enabling our faith communities to reach out with love, understanding, and support, so that healing for deeply wounded people might become a more realized possibility.

References

Bolton I: *My Son... My Son...* Atlanta, The Bolton Press, 1983.

Buechner F: *Telling Secrets: A Memoir.* San Francisco, HarperCollins Publishers, 1991.

Clemons JT: *What Does the Bible Say About Suicide?* Minneapolis, Augsburg Fortress, 1990.

Colt GC: The history of the suicide survivor: The Mark of Cain. In Dunne EJ, McIntosh JL, Dunne-Maxim K (editors): *Suicide and Its Aftermath*. New York, W.W. Norton & Co., 1987, pages 3-18.

Nouwen HJM: *The Wounded Healer*. Garden City, NY, Doubleday & Co., Inc., 1972.

Wolfelt AD: *Death and Grief: A Guide for Clergy*. Muncie, IN, Accelerated Development, Inc., 1988.

Chapter 12

Supporting the Family After a Suicide

Rabbi Robert J. Marx, Ph.D.

Start with a sense of the holy. To be holy is not merely to be religious. It is to be aware of the awesomeness of separation and of coming together. The Hebrew word for Holy, *Kadosh*, implies both of these acts. The Sabbath begins with the lighting of the candles and the chanting of Kiddush, the prayer of sanctification. The candle symbolizes the separation of day from night, of work from holy rest, and the Kiddush prayer, pronounced over the wine, gives historic sanction to this separating and reuniting process.

Every tradition has its rituals of separation and re-dedication. That which is holy separates and then returns in a new and transformed way. That which is holy separates from the everyday and creates the Sabbath, separates from mother and father and creates a marriage, separates from death and creates a new dedication to life.

At a time of suicide, the family needs an awareness of the holy. It needs to feel that the shattering of so many values may yet lead to wholeness. And the clergyperson trying to help needs to feel the potential of the holy as he/she tries to bring light where there is darkness, and hope where there is despair.

The awareness of the death is the first challenge. The family is in chaos. The minister or priest or rabbi is called either because of closeness to the family or because of his/her official role. The task is to arrange for the funeral. But at a time of suicide more is needed than a funeral. The total involvement of the cleric is required.

And so the first challenge calls forth questions that demand resolution. They are questions that every clergyperson must ask of him/herself before beginning to help. They are questions which require honesty and no small measure of courage. How do I feel about the task I have been asked to undertake? What does my tradition say about suicide, and how can I reconcile my role as a comforter with my responsibilities to my faith? Can I find the words of comfort, the deeds of reconciliation that will honestly allow me to maintain my dual role as a comforter and as a spokesman for my tradition? Of course, by dealing with these questions even before a crisis occurs, we may avoid the ambiguities that so often shadow us. But for many of us, the act of reconciliation is one that must be undertaken afresh with each suicide we confront.

I confess that every completed suicide is an act of confrontation for me. I admit that I cannot stand in the place of the Creator and demand of my children that they "choose life." The act of suicide is a frightening affirmation that human beings may still choose, even though they may not choose the answer that tradition demands. That affirmation can produce terrifying results, results that have devastating consequences for an entire family as well as for an entire community.

In the face of a completed suicide I must confront my own fear. Fear that I may not have answers where answers are expected. Fear that I may not be able to help where help is so desperately needed. I spend a great deal of time helping families who have experienced the loss of a child. I can say to them: "I know how you feel. I have lost a child." But I cannot say to the family of a suicide: "I know how you feel." For I do not know — and in this acknowledgment, perhaps I can begin to help with a little more humility and a great deal more integrity.

If confronting my fear evokes the separation inherent in the holy, it is important for me to do more than remain suspended in doubt. The act of holy returning is to be found in the consciousness that I am expected to help. My experience and my training prepare me for the act of helping. The act cannot be evaded. It remains for my faith and my love of God to help me enter a new moment, one of healing and of hope.

For some suicides, the completion of the act is the culmination of years of pain and suffering. For some family members after a suicide, the suicide of the one they love comes as no surprise. But they are the exception. For most, the completion of a suicide plunges the survivors into chaos. Family and friends are devastated. The clergyperson enters a scene where rational values have been stood on their head. Parents who lose a child tell me that the loss causes them to grow a "little crazy." So, too, the survivors in a family where there is a suicide become a "little crazy."

It is important, then, to enter into the world of those survivors, and to listen to their perceptions. It is important to really hear the words of their child, their wife, their father, as they, the survivors, remember the one they loved. This is not a time for the clergyperson to analyze the conditions that lead to the completed act, or to offer a biography or a diagnosis of mental illness. Rather the cleric is most helpful by being able to listen and to comfort. Family and friends may all offer their verdicts. What is most needed is not judgment but a holy consolation, one that offers comforting love rather than incisive diagnosis.

The funeral represents a special challenge to those who would help. Here, the private and public aspects of the cleric must be brought together, if not totally harmonized. Suicide is not an act to be glamorized. It is an act born of illness or despair. To remind the survivors of their beloved, it is not necessary to glorify the suicide. For impressionable teen-agers as well as for suggestive adults, it is all too easy to lend a dark glamour to the suicide — a glamour which can only prove disastrous.

There are no formulas. Every life is unique. I urge clergypersons planning the funeral of a suicide to avoid the feeling that a message which is helpful on one occasion may be universally useful. We know that words that are comforting for some are abrasive to others, just as words that can be spoken by some become anathema when spoken by others. The uniqueness and authenticity of each life needs to be understood, and encompassed by the eulogy.

The liturgy may be helpful. It may also be disappointing. A favorite psalm, a familiar poem, may offer great comfort. But it is not inappropriate to innovate in dealing with the funeral of a suicide. The need for innovation can become particularly urgent because so many traditional liturgies simply do not deal with the problem of suicide. Many of these liturgies assume that everyone leads a full creative life. Such liturgies offer little comfort to the relatives of someone who has suffered so much.

Because of this disappointment in the liturgy, a funeral service which dares to be very personal may also succeed in being the most helpful. A beloved piece of music, a letter written by the suicide or to him/her, a poem or piece of art work displayed at the funeral — any one of these may be comforting symbols of the life that is being remembered.

I am reluctant to take the funeral of a suicide away from the customary sites for such ceremonies — a house of worship or a funeral home. Remembering someone in a place of special memory, on a favorite hillside or beside a pool of water, must avoid the scylla of glamorizing the manner of the death and the charybdis of removing the ceremony from the places where we normally bury our dead and console the survivors. At the same time, these special places can bring to the mourners a sense of sanity and familiarity that are sometimes lacking in a funeral home or house of worship.

The words are important. But they are not to be found in formulas. A God who comforts is not to be found in slogans, but in a living encounter with the tragedy of the moment. For some, it may be consoling to suggest that God so loved Suzy that He took her to be His own. My experience, however, has been that most mature adults look for a God who does not take life, but who gives it; who does not punish, but who offers redemption and salvation.

A time of death can be a time of anger — and so, very often, God is a primary recipient of that anger. How could God do this to me? I recognize that each tradition has its own theology of comfort and its own stories of comfort to tell, but I feel that the reconciling role of the clergy must deflect the view that what has happened is a form of God's punishment. Rather, it should include a view of a God who allows us to grow and deal with our losses. Some gain comfort in the conviction that the dead live in the memory of those who love them. Others are convinced that they live on with God and will experience a resurrection in the future. These issues are not to be dismissed lightly, for they become especially urgent at a time when chaos and despair seem so pervasive.

How can the cleric best help? By recognizing that the funeral is the beginning and not the end of the comforting role. So many people come to the survivors and say: "It has been six weeks or three months. It is time to put an end to your mourning, to return to normalcy." But for the survivors of a suicide there is no normalcy and, characteristically, no end to the mourning. The guilt, the anger, and the sense of loss often persist for months or years. If I have learned one thing about grief, it is that there can be no timetable for mourning. And suicide leaves behind so many shattered hopes and so many unanswered questions that even the pressure to return to "normalcy" becomes an impediment to this goal.

To be sure in Judaism, as in many other faiths, there are time periods in which the mourning process occurs. *Shiva* means seven and it is the seven-day period of severest mourning which follows on the heels of the death. This is succeeded by the *Sheloshim*, or thirty, the first month where the mourning is less intense than during the first seven days. And finally there is the *yahrzeit*, the time at the end of the first year of mourning when the formal rites of remembrance are concluded. All of these ceremonies speak of time, but they should be understood as guides to help one return to normal routines, rather than to a "normal" frame of mind.

The clergyperson who would really help must be aware of the artificiality of all time schedules. The helping process should continue long after the funeral itself. Even a family picnic on the anniversary of the death may be a comforting act for some survivors who would retain their happy memories. A day in the country, a favorite song or movie, a visit to the cemetery — all of these may be acts that reduce the pain and allow friends and family to comfort one another.

It remains to point out some of the additional problems that a cleric may confront in the process of consolation and healing. As in any traumatic act of separation, pathologies may occur, and a wise clergyperson can help a family find perspective as they deal with their tragedy. Some of these pathologies will require professional help; others can be dealt with at a pastoral level.

The Bible suggests that the brothers of Joseph knew that their youngest brother, Benjamin, was the favorite of Jacob, their father.

Benjamin, like Joseph, was the son of the beloved wife, Rachel. Having been told that Joseph died, Jacob lavished his attention on Benjamin. This was a family where jealously among siblings produced historic consequences. So too, in a family where a suicide occurs, the overprotection of a surviving child or children may produce a stifling impact. The result may be children who are afraid to grow on their own or take the risks necessary to achieve mature adulthood. Can the religious community help?

What of the opposite patterns? The dead member of the family becomes so idolized that the surviving siblings are made to feel inadequate and unloved. Death has a way of erasing criticism. The toll upon those who survive may be more than their sense of loss. It may produce guilt that they survived while their sister died, or a feeling that they can never live up to the idealized vision of a sister who has suddenly become endowed with divine dimensions. Can the religious community help?

And can we help the survivors emerge from the social isolation which so often follows a suicide? Fear, anger, guilt — these are the emotions which so often adhere to the survivors, and make it difficult, if not impossible, for them to return to a healthy social environment. To accept their anger, to understand their guilt, to provide situations where their embarrassment may be assuaged, these too are the tasks of the religious community.

Martin Buber tells a moving story of a student who came to him one day with a simple question. At the time, Buber was teaching social philosophy at the University of Frankfurt, and the simple question was: "Shall I take a course in Biology or in Botany?" Without thinking, Buber gave an off-hand answer. Weeks later the student took his own life. Buber tells us that after this tragedy occurred he realized that the student's question, far from being merely academic, was a life question. And Buber had failed to penetrate its depths and to really listen. The life of dialogue begins with the ability to really listen.

In a time of darkest despair, the religious comforter is faced with the responsibility of entering into the deep shadow of life's most tragic moment. To confront death itself, to listen to the survivors, to bring the holy into this world — this is the challenge. This is the opportunity.

Chapter 13

The Role of the Clergy for Survivors of Suicide

Father Charles T. Rubey, L.C.S.W.

The role of the clergy is very important in working with someone who has lost a loved one to suicide. In most instances, people turn to a clergyperson first for comfort and consolation. They need to be reassured that they are not "unclean" or "tainted." Surviving family members may feel they are being negatively judged in social or professional circles — as being failed parents, spouses, children, or siblings. To help combat these feelings as well as the usual feelings of grief, the clergyperson will be called upon to fill a number of roles. We are expected to be sources of hope and support, aides in the creation of memorial rituals, and guides through the grieving process.

The primary role of the clergyperson in the case of suicide is that of *nonjudgmental* supporter and nurturer. Because for centuries suicide was placed in the moral sphere, clergy should evaluate their own attitude toward suicide before taking on this role. Our attitudes will come across quite clearly to the grieving person. Often people grieving the death of a suicide already feel that they have done wrong or are "stained." If the clergy reinforces these negative feelings in surviving family members, grief work and the healing process are rendered more difficult. Clergy must ask themselves basic questions such as: "What is my attitude toward suicide? Do I think that suicide is a sin? Do I think that people who have completed suicide are condemned to hell? Do I think that people who have completed suicide are sinners?"

My own attitude formed gradually as I was able to take suicide out of the realm of morality and place it into the medical realm where it belongs. I believe the problem of suicide to be analogous to that of alcoholism insofar as alcoholism has evolved from a moral into a medical issue. A person completes suicide because he/she is in such desperate straits that this fatal act becomes the only way to relieve the intense pain. It is a final act of desperation. I believe that God does not judge a person negatively when a person acts out of desperation. He only condemns when a person acts out of malice. People who complete suicide are not malicious, they are desperate. Survivors look to clergy to reinforce the fact that their loved ones are at peace and not in hell. The clergy are anchors of hope for these survivors. For people who believe in an after-life, the clergy act as links to the life hereafter. By his/her role, the clergyperson can instill hope in the grieving person.

Another role the clergy must assume is that of presider over rituals. Planning the funeral is an important process, and clergy can play an integral part in guiding family and friends in this first ritual for the deceased. The funeral should not glamorize a suicide but should be a final statement about the person's life and death. Clergypersons should also encourage families to create other rituals that commemorate important days in the life of the deceased. Such rituals provide a healthy forum for people to gather and remember their beloved dead. Rituals can be religious or secular, and can be something as simple as drinking a glass of wine together, or as elaborate as a Mass or other type of prayer service.

Rituals are a gathering point for a family to acknowledge that a significant person has left their midst. Even when people die, the reality of their life remains an integral part of a family or group of people. With a suicide, the key survivors feel guilty that they have let the person down in life. The greatest fear of the grieving is that the loved one will be forgotten. This would make the person's death a doubly tragic event. Rituals allow people to maintain contact with their beloved dead through thought and prayer. Rituals reinforce the idea that, while this person is no longer among the living, he/she is remembered as part of a family — part of a system of people.

Survivors should be encouraged to celebrate key dates in the deceased person's life such as birthdays, the anniversary of death,

Thanksgiving, or Christmas. These rituals do not necessarily have to be presided over by a member of the clergy, but clergy can act as a resource in their preparation. Certain days lend themselves naturally to becoming ritual occasions — days such as the anniversary of death or special holidays.

Birthdays tend to be more awkward for the survivors. Memories of prior light-hearted birthday gatherings may be difficult to recall and tolerate. When a person has died — especially a tragic death like a suicide — the birth date is a painful reminder of happy celebrations of the past. For this very reason, I think it is most appropriate to have some form of a ritual on the date of the birth in an attempt to alleviate the pain of these kinds of memories. The worst thing that can happen would be to treat this day like any other day. People need to know it is okay to have a ritual on the birth date of their loved one even though the person is no longer living. When the purpose of the gathering is properly understood and communicated, the ritual can actually be an effective agent of healing. Thus a family might clarify: "This is not a birthday party. This is a way to remember that a significant person was born on this day and, while the person is no longer among the living, his/her birthday is still an important day in the life of our family or friends who are left to mourn his/her absence." A ritual is a way to remember that the deceased person is alive in thoughts and prayers and thus in the ritual itself.

A third role of the clergyperson is to be a patient and loyal guide through the grieving process. Clergy must remember that the grief experience is often lengthy and painful for those involved. In circles of extended family and friends, people expect the grieving person to move on very quickly with their everyday lives. In this case, the role of the clergy is to allow people to grieve sufficiently and thoroughly. It is comforting to people when clergy ask how they are coping and show genuine concern about the grieving person's welfare. Those we serve have come to expect this type of caring from their clergyperson. What makes suicide a unique experience is that there are no answers as to why the person died. Survivors want answers and will look to their clergy for them. They will ask clergy direct questions and will expect direct answers. Many survivors lose confidence in their clergy or their religion at this point, in response to a careless or poorly deliberated theological answer or an answer that fails to recognize their personal pathos and pain. Since there are no definitive answers to the many questions regarding suicide, such questions remain unanswered. A clergyperson must not be afraid to be frank about this reality.

All around them, survivors hear pious and insipid platitudes. For example, if a couple has lost one child to suicide and they have four remaining children, they will constantly hear: "You're fortunate that you have four other children." This kind of comment is intended to be helpful, but it can be very painful. The parents find such remarks offensive, because they are concentrating on the loss of the one child. Similarly, if a man has lost his wife, he is probably not ready to hear that he can get married again. These are both examples of how outsiders try to sugar-coat and minimize the grieving experience. It is important that clergy do not follow suit but are forthright in their dealings with parishioners instead. Survivors have a right to expect a realistic approach to the grief experience from their clergy. They need honesty and direct behavior. This grieving period is an extremely painful time in the survivor's life, and it will take a long time for him/her to learn to live with the pain. Survivors are aware that outsiders are uncomfortable with the pain they are experiencing. This can make them feel like a pariah in many sectors of society. It is important that clergy do not reinforce these feelings. Straightforward behavior on the part of the clergyperson is the best solution to this problem.

Because they are guides through the grieving process, people may look to their clergy for ways to short-cut through the grief experience. However, this is impossible; there is no easy way through the grief. In order for a person to have any kind of hopeful future, it is imperative that the survivor feel and process the pain of the entire experience. Clergy have the opportunity to assist parishioners in this task. They can be both guiding light and anchor of hope as their parishioners go from the darkness of the grief experience to the dawn of a different type of life. The survivors will never be the same because the grief experience leaves lasting residues throughout their lives.

We as clergy are called upon to play a variety of roles as our parishioners journey through the grieving process. We must be supportive and nurturing, helpful in the creation of rituals, and loyal guides. We can perform a service if we have a realistic and honest approach to the grief experience. Though we act as the caretakers of people's lives, this in no way implies that we must be a shield or protective force for them. Certain events are devastating, and suicide is only one of these experiences. We have a golden opportunity to hold the hands of the survivors and guide them through this painful time.

VI. Spirituality and Mental Health

Introduction

Are depression and suicidal despair nothing more than evidence of separation from God, in the sense that piety and prayer can be recommended as sufficient and complete therapies? If, on the other hand, depressive illness and suicidal symptoms have their roots in genetic predisposition and alterations of brain neurochemistry, does spiritual counseling have any value in these conditions? If the "spiritual" and "psychopathological" dimensions of suicidal despair overlap in specific cases, how should one integrate spiritual and mental health therapeutics?

These provocative questions define the scope of this section. Chapter 14 represents a probing analysis of the relationship between pastoral and mental health care. Dr. Fitchett, Rev. Ashby, and Rev. Groh discuss three case illustrations, describing the themes of estrangement, abandonment, betrayal, isolation, and conflicted relations with significant others — including God and church — that characterize many suicidal persons. They outline a model for deciding which suicidal persons require little more than the support of a congregational community, which benefit from pastoral counseling, and which require psychiatric care coordinated with pastoral care.

In Chapter 15, Dr. Holinger provides several case illustrations to make the point that an important clinical tool, the *mental status examination*, can provide the cleric with information that helps him/her identify which persons require psychiatric services.

Chapter 14

The Boundary Between Pastoral and Mental Health Care

George Fitchett, D.Min.,
Rev. Homer U. Ashby, Jr., Ph.D., and
Rev. Lucille Sider Groh, Ph.D.

Introduction

The question addressed in this chapter is: How are pastoral care and mental health care related in the care of suicidal persons? To begin with, three disguised cases will be presented in which pastoral caregivers worked with suicidal persons. This case material will provide the basis for a discussion about the relationship and possible boundaries between pastoral care and mental health care with suicidal persons.

I. The case of Jane

Jane is a 34-year-old woman who began pastoral psychotherapy about six years ago. At the time she said she felt suicidal because of a recent breakup with a boyfriend. Although her suicidal feelings were strong, there was no suicide plan. Suicide did not seem to be the primary issue at the end of the first session.

Jane had made one suicide attempt years before, at the age of ten, when she was angry with her mother. She took pills from the medicine cabinet and told her brother she had done so. She was rushed to the hospital and her stomach was pumped. Since that time, she has had strong suicidal thoughts at times of high stress but has not made any more suicide attempts.

During her current therapy two underlying issues have been explored in great depth. The first is the fact that Jane felt abandoned by both her parents. She was the youngest in a family of twelve. Her mother worked full-time and had very little energy for her. She was raised by her older siblings. Her father was more nurturing than her mother, but he died when she was thirteen years old. In the midst of this, from ages seven to fourteen, she was sexually molested by her uncle. Thus, themes of abandonment, lack of nurture, and sexual abuse have been the primary issues which have been explored in the pastoral psychotherapy.

Two other issues have emerged more recently. The first is that of weight gain and weight loss. Jane's pattern has been to lose weight when single or when dating, when without a partner; then to gain a great deal of weight when she is married or when she has a steady partner. She gains up to 30 or 40 pounds. It is as if she cannot tolerate the intensity of the relationship, so she eats as a way of making herself unattractive. This serves the purpose of distancing herself and is a way of abandoning herself and her partner.

The other set of issues that has been explored is her religious experiences. She was raised Roman Catholic and went to Roman Catholic schools. She had mainly negative experiences with her teachers there, but she had one teacher, a nun, who believed in her and treated her kindly. That nurturing experience was pivotal for her. In her teens she left the Roman Catholic Church, joined a Baptist Church and became, in her own words, a "Jesus freak." She was very involved in Bible studies, witnessing, and other activities. At age 19, she replaced religion with sex and became quite promiscuous. This continued on and off throughout the years, although not when married. She is currently married and living in a monogamous relationship. She speaks rather bitterly about each of her encounters with religion, both as a Roman Catholic and as a Baptist. Her religious experiences were just touched on intermittently through the first years of therapy.

About six months ago Jane began a session with a direct and rather unusual question, "Do you think there is anything I need to deal with or explore to further my healing?" It came up suddenly. Her counselor paused and responded directly, "Yes, I believe there is something else. I believe you need to find yourself in relation to God. I believe wholeness involves a relationship to God and wholeness is what you are seeking. I believe wholeness involves a relationship with God as well as a good relationship with others. I am aware you have had very painful and destructive experiences in the church, yet I believe your wholeness will include finding a relationship to God through all of that."

Jane then talked for a long time about feeling abandoned by God. This reminded her counselor of the Psalms and the feelings of abandonment by God expressed there. The therapist quoted some of those passages to Jane. It also brought back memories of their first years of therapy and Jane's feelings of abandonment by her mother and father. Jane launched into periods of great anger about the way she felt abandoned by God and also by the Church. The counselor listened to this empathically, never defending the church, never defending God, and not arguing with her.

Jane tried to abandon the counselor several times during their work. She took two long breaks, one when she was angry because she felt the counselor was not helping her with her weight problem. The counselor gladly received her back into therapy each time she sought to return. Not abandoning her is a way in which Jane's feelings of abandonment are gradually being healed. This is also laying the foundation for Jane to open herself to God.

Suicide may be understood as an act that comes from feeling utterly abandoned. The counselor believes Jane will not commit suicide because she is finding people who are not abandoning her and she is abandoning herself less and less. The counselor also believes that in the future Jane will find security in God. It will likely take several years, but there is no rush.

II. The case of Ethel

The chaplain first met Ethel, age 66, over four years ago. At that time she was a patient on the adult general psychiatric unit at the hospital. Ethel is a Caucasian woman of Canadian and English descent. Her husband, Victor, had died the previous winter, just nine months prior to her hospitalization. At the time of his death, Ethel and Victor had been married just a week short of 40 years.

Ethel and Victor have one adopted daughter, Karen. Ethel's relationship with Karen was at that time quite strained. It improved later. Karen has one daughter, named Veronica, by her first marriage. Ethel and Veronica have a better relationship than Ethel and Karen. At the time of the initial counseling meetings, Veronica was a high school student. On the way home from high school she would periodically stop at Ethel's house and visit with her grandmother and see how she was doing.

Ethel lives in the home that she and Victor owned in an affluent suburb. She has lived there for many years and been active in many community and civic groups, especially in the American Legion Auxiliary. Ethel has been the President of that organization on several occasions.

Ethel and Victor were active in a local Protestant church. In the years prior to Victor's death they did not get out to church much. They were a "shut-in" couple. The pastor and members of the church would come and visit and contact was maintained that way. Ethel is remembered by the former pastor of the church with a great deal of warmth. Obviously, he felt very close to both Ethel and Victor. The current pastor had gotten to know both Ethel and Victor and developed a similarly warm relationship with them.

Ethel suffers from several physical health problems. She has been an insulin-dependent diabetic for ten years. She had intestinal cancer twelve years ago. The cancer seems to have been successfully treated with surgery. She has an ilio-conduit as a result of that surgery. She also has some chronic arthritis and back pain for which she takes medication.

Ethel's hospitalization in the fall of 1986 was the first of three psychiatric hospitalizations. It actually began on a medical unit. Ethel came to the hospital because her diabetes was out of control. Attempts to adjust her medication to control her diabetes were not successful. In the course of her medical hospitalization Ethel was found to be severely depressed, with suicidal ideation. She was transferred to the psychiatric unit.

The issue that came into focus in that first psychiatric hospitalization was whether Ethel's medical condition was so unstable that she would not be able to return to live at home independently. Ethel was very upset when she was informed of that possibility. The thought of moving to a nursing home, losing the home she and Victor had, caused great distress for her. She was also depressed and grieving the end of the marriage to Victor. She was not sure if there was anything she wanted to live for.

During the hospitalization, Ethel worked on her grief over the loss of Victor, and she demonstrated some resolve to go on living. Her depression improved somewhat with medication and therapy. Suicidal ideation diminished and was no longer a problem. Further changes in her medication led to the stabilization of her diabetes. Ethel was discharged from the hospital after four weeks with plans to continue seeing her psychiatrist for medication as an outpatient.

Her local pastor provided great support around the discharge planning. Throughout Ethel's hospitalization he had said that if it was hard for Ethel to live at home alone, he and the people of the church would come in every day to do what was necessary to assist her. He was frequently at the hospital to visit with Ethel and keep her connected with the church and to pray with her.

During the first hospitalization, the chaplain was only modestly involved in care for Ethel. The chaplain facilitated some expression of grief over Victor's death and helped Ethel try to find meaning in life without Victor. The chaplain assisted in integrating the pastor into the treatment team and helping the treatment team view him as an important resource in this case. The chaplain prayed with Ethel.

To the chaplain's surprise, after her discharge, Ethel kept in contact with the chaplain. She periodically called the chaplain to say that she was doing fine and that she was keeping up with her appointments. She said she was finding some meaning in living and was doing all right.

Fourteen months later Ethel had a second crisis. Her granddaughter Veronica had become pregnant. Veronica's mother, Karen, had thrown her out of the house and did not want to have anything to do with her. Veronica had come to live with Ethel in the basement apartment of Ethel's house where Karen had once lived with her husband. Veronica and her boyfriend now moved into that apartment. The whole extended family was in a state of crisis and chaos. Ethel asked the chaplain to assist in finding a clinic which would provide prenatal care for Veronica, and family therapy for Veronica, Karen and Ethel. The chaplain was not successful in efforts to locate resources which the family could afford. A clinic which provided prenatal care was finally located by Ethel, using her own network of friends and contacts in the community.

A month later, just a few days after Christmas, Ethel called and said that she thought things would be better if she were gone. There had been an argument in the family. Ethel was beginning to set some rules about behavior for Veronica and her boyfriend. The boyfriend had complained about these rules. Karen had said to Ethel, "It will be your fault if Veronica's boyfriend leaves her."

There had been plans for a Christmas dinner together at Ethel's house. A wonderful, warm family holiday time together was planned. Instead there had been a big argument. The dinner did not happen. The members of the family fought with each other on Christmas. Several days later Ethel was feeling depressed and suicidal. She called the chaplain. She had already called her friends and the pastor. She talked about feeling that everyone would be better off if she were gone. The day before New Year's Eve, she took an overdose of her pain medication. The pastor brought her to the emergency room and she was hospitalized again.

The focus of this hospitalization was a little different than the first. It now seemed important to begin to sort out the family dynamics that appeared to be linked to this episode. A social worker worked with Veronica and her boyfriend and also with Karen and Ethel. Ethel was initially resistant to family therapy. She thought that talking about things in the family would only make the problems worse. The staff did not think things could get much worse and encouraged Ethel to try therapy.

The staff also tried to get Ethel to focus more on her own life. They tried to help Ethel see that there were a lot of problems that Veronica was having with which Ethel could not help; Veronica would have to deal with them herself. Ethel needed to find some activities and interests for her life separate from Veronica's life. The staff talked with Ethel about what she might want to get involved with, and Ethel began to think about that and make some plans. Ethel was discharged after four weeks with a referral for follow-up family therapy at a family mental health clinic where the pastor served on the board. Ethel was also encouraged to pursue some of her own activities and to continue with her medications and visits with her psychiatrist.

During Ethel's second hospitalization the chaplain took a bit more active role in trying to suggest to the treatment team that family system issues were important to deal with in addition to Ethel's depression. The chaplain argued that the team needed to look at the whole family system while at the same time remaining supportive to Ethel personally during the hospitalization. The chaplain also stressed the importance of helping Ethel focus on her own activities — what her life was going to be about if she was not going to be over-involved in her family's lives.

Things went fairly well for Ethel in the months that followed. She was exploring some new activities. Family relationships were improving. They made some efforts to engage in outpatient family therapy, but basically that did not work out.

Just two days after Easter, Ethel called the chaplain again and said she was leaving town and not planning to come back. She had a kidney infection and she was not going to take any medication for it. She did not want to hurt anymore, did not know what to do, and wanted to die. There had been another family argument, this time between Ethel and Karen, over the baby shower and who was going to buy what. The plans for an Easter dinner for the family had not materialized because of the big family argument. Four days after Easter, Ethel was back in the hospital.

During this hospitalization there was more focus on Ethel's suicidal ideation. She was also less cooperative with the unit's rules than she had been during previous hospitalizations. For example, she tested limits and rules about where she was allowed to go on the unit. She seemed to be making gestures related to escaping from the unit. She was confined in seclusion on two occasions for failure to cooperate with the staff and follow rules related to where she was allowed to be. Overall it was a different hospitalization for Ethel than her previous ones had been.

Gradually, with adjustments in her medication and continued milieu treatment, Ethel's behavior improved. The family conflict seemed to diminish. Ethel's sense of self-worth was improving. She was discharged with a referral for outpatient pastoral counseling. It was suggested that she continue to work on the way she handled her anger in the family and also to look at how she handled issues of anger and conflict.

During the third hospitalization the chaplain felt it was important for Ethel to deal with some of the grief that seemed to be present and also with feelings of anger toward God for all the terrible things that had befallen her. The chaplain told Ethel that it was important for her not to hold all these feelings in, but to express them. Later the chaplain felt that these suggestions had not been too helpful. They seemed to have increased Ethel's anxiety and may have been part of why she was not cooperating well with the rest of the treatment team. The chaplain discontinued that approach and supported the style of management and structuring of feelings which was being encouraged by the rest of the treatment team. This approach seemed to work out well.

One month after her discharge from the third hospitalization, Ethel's great-granddaughter was born. Ethel saw the pastoral counselor she was referred to twice. After her great-granddaughter was born she stopped seeing the pastoral counselor. She has not been involved in any other counseling since then. Ethel has not had any further suicidal ideation or thoughts since the baby's birth. Her mood is vastly improved and her sense of meaning in life is dramatically sustained by caring for her great-granddaughter, who lives with her.

Life for Ethel has not been without problems since the baby's birth, and so her sustained improved mood is all the more remarkable. She has been in the hospital several times for various medical conditions and also has had some outpatient surgery. Her medical problems are numerous but none of that has affected her mood. Eight months after her great-granddaughter was born she was at the hospital for an eye appointment. The chaplain went to see her. She told the chaplain that one of the things that gives her great meaning is rocking the baby to sleep. As she does this she says to the baby, "You and I have a little secret, because you saved my life and I saved yours." The first reference appears easy to understand. The child's birth has given Ethel a renewed sense of meaning and purpose in life. The second reference appears to refer to the fact that Ethel intervened when early in Veronica's pregnancy one of the options being discussed was for Veronica to have an abortion.

III. The case of James and Mary

James and Mary had known each other for seven years. It had been a stormy relationship with frequent breakups and separations. Their most recent break-up occurred three months before James committed suicide.

The couple had come for pastoral counseling to see if they could patch things up. In the counseling James expressed extreme anger and rage at Mary because of her emotional distance. He was insightful enough to realize that he wanted Mary to be close to him like his mother was. He could not handle the emotional distance that Mary maintained. Mary was frightened of James. In the past he had been physically and emotionally abusive. She did not want to endure the abuse but also felt sorry for James and did not want to leave him. In counseling it became clearer to Mary that she did not want to continue the relationship with James. As she began to reveal these feelings in the sessions James became enraged. He began to spy on her, steal her mail, physically assault her, and cut the brake lines on her car. Presented with this set of circumstances, the pastoral counselor counseled Mary to keep her distance from James and to employ the police if necessary.

James was also in individual counseling at the time. The pastoral counselor consulted with James' individual therapist about her assessment of James' potential for danger to himself and others. She indicated that if the relationship with Mary ended, such danger was a real possibility. The pastoral counselor told James' therapist that he was planning on bringing the couple counseling to an end. The pastoral counselor thought it was more of a destructive than a helpful process. James' therapist said that she hoped the termination of the couple's counseling would not also be a termination in the relationship between James and Mary. The pastoral counselor told her that it was not his decision whether the relationship continued or not. The pastoral counselor also said that it was not clear that continuing the relationship was the best thing for either James or Mary.

Once confronted by Mary, James wrote a long letter of apology. It was addressed to Mary and other members of his family whom he felt he had hurt. This is the letter:

> *This is a letter of apology to all whom I've hurt, disappointed, or in other ways caused discomfort. Although my apology is sincere, I have no expectations of you forgiving me. I'm especially sorry for what I've done to Mary and my son. The following is not an excuse but rather an explanation of why I've acted so terribly. I have for years been consumed with anger and fear. These emotions interfered with the establishment and maintenance of healthy and loving relationships. I tended to psychoanalyze others into believing that the fault was entirely theirs. My two major areas of fault lie in fostering a general climate of hostility and indirect verbal and physical attack. These are inexcusable. For those of you who have suffered the most and yet remained with me, I can only surmise that either you are grand fools or your love for me has been great enough to focus on what good there is in me. I ask from those who still love me that you no longer accept or tolerate my problems. I intend to work hard at solving my problems. One way you can help is by telling me to wash my face whenever you detect that I'm not controlling my anger. If I return still angry — tell me to do it again. If that's to no avail, then tell me to get the hell away from you until I can control myself. The responsibility is mine. I seek only assistance for those times when I may be blind to what is happening with me. Because this letter is addressed to so many people I could only address general faults. I am more than willing to provide you with specific apologies. Along with my apology is a pledge to not do as I have in the past. For those of you who have already given up on me, I offer my understanding. For those of you who might be cautiously considering resurrecting a relationship with me, I offer patience. For those of you who continue to love me, I offer my thanks. I am sorry. (He signed his name).*

James' letter sits on the boundary. It can be read as a suicide letter or it can be read as a request for forgiveness and a desire to engage in a healing process of reconciliation. James entered the hospital the day after delivering the letter. Mary visited him there and found him confused and irrational. Without any severe signs of psychosis or bizarre behavior, James was allowed to sign himself out after two days' stay in the hospital. Two days later James committed suicide.

In this particular case the pastoral counselor struggled with the question of whether to be attentive to the pastoral care issues of helping to heal a troubled relationship or attentive to the mental illness issues of one of the relationship's partners. From a pastoral care perspective the pastoral counselor focused on how to bring about better communication between James and Mary, how to help them see what each contributed to the problems in the relationship, and how to facilitate their efforts to address their problems as a couple. Issues of joint responsibility and forgiveness would dominate the work with them. If the pastoral counselor's focus was on mental illness or mental health care, then the pastoral counselor's attention would be drawn to James whose potential for suicide and homicide required intervention from an external authority, an authority who would provide healing and protection to a person who was increasingly out of control. In retrospect the pastoral counselor feels that more of a mental health approach than a pastoral care approach was taken. The pastoral counselor decided to forego the pastoral care and focus on the relationship in order to address the mental health concern for James.

IV. General discussion

As the cases illustrate, the relation between pastoral care and mental health care with suicidal persons may be quite different in different cases. Two factors seem most significant in shaping these differences: the severity of the suicidal ideation or behavior and the context in which the pastoral care or counseling takes place. By context we mean the setting in which the pastoral care is provided. In our three case illustrations, for example, the context of care for Jane and James was a pastoral counseling center. For Ethel the contexts were the parish and the hospital. The context gives shape to the specific role and associated expectations for the pastoral care giver.

In the following discussion we will first focus on the relation between pastoral care and mental health care in non-acute cases of suicide. Then we will elaborate on the relation in cases of acute suicidal ideation and behavior. For both of these topics, we will explore the relation in all three contexts for ministry, the parish, the pastoral counseling center and the hospital.

At the beginning there are two general comments we wish to make. First, our differences in pastoral context notwithstanding, each of us initially responded to the invitation to contribute to this book by saying that our contact with suicidal persons was infrequent or non-existent. On second thought, we began to recall cases where suicide had been an issue. What does this mean? Minimally it suggests that suicide is not an obvious feature in the pastoral practice in the settings and the populations with which we work. But perhaps suicide is more present than we tend to recognize.

Second, when we looked at all three cases we realized that estrangement was a significant feature in each. Each case contained an account of frustrated efforts to establish meaningful interpersonal relationships or community. This link between suicidal behavior and community is evident, for example, in Ethel's case. When her husband of forty years died she became depressed and suicidal and was hospitalized. Her second and third hospitalizations and associated suicidal behavior were precipitated by family arguments. Her psychiatric condition, her mental health, was dramatically improved by the birth of her great granddaughter and her active involvement in the care of that child.

V. The relation between pastoral and mental health care in non-acute cases

Two of our cases, Jane and Ethel, help us explore the relation between pastoral care and mental health care in non-acute suicidal cases. In Jane's case all of her care has been pastoral care. We know of no mental health care that she has received. Her pastoral counselor assessed the level of risk associated with Jane's suicidal thoughts and behavior, and judged that pastoral counseling would be helpful to Jane.

What about the parish as a context for pastoral care for Jane? She has had no contact with any parish as an adult. As a child she was raised Catholic. Her memories focus mainly on the negative experiences of parochial school. One nurturing nun was an exception. As an adolescent she was, as she says, "a Jesus freak" and involved in a Baptist church, Bible study, and witnessing. She remembers this period, like her time as a Catholic, with bitterness.

Her pastoral counselor shared with Jane a belief that wholeness includes a relationship with God. The counselor told Jane that as she seeks wholeness she will seek a relationship with God. Jane and her counselor have explored this, and Jane's feelings of being abandoned by God were a focus of their attention. Further healing for Jane focused on feelings of abandonment. As this healing occurs, perhaps Jane will be ready to explore participation in a parish which for her might be a community of the knowledge and love of a faithful God, and a community of love and care for one another.

Ethel's case seems quite different from Jane's. It contains acute episodes of suicidal ideation, suicidal behavior, and psychiatric hospitalization. It also contains extended periods where there was no suicidal behavior or ideation. At this point in our discussion we want to explore the latter periods. After her first hospitalization, Ethel received mental health care. She saw her psychiatrist on an outpatient basis for medication for her depression. She also received pastoral care. She received pastoral support from the pastor of her parish and also, more infrequently, from the hospital chaplain. A similar pattern was established after her second hospitalization. In contrast to Jane, Ethel needed the support of medication in addition to pastoral care, even in non-acute periods. Unlike Jane, she was not interested in any in-depth therapeutic exploration of her troublesome feelings, relationships, or their history in her life.

Ethel's case highlights the significant role the local congregation and pastor can play in care for a suicidal person during non-acute periods of their illness. The pastor and members of the congregation stayed connected with Ethel, minimizing her feelings of isolation and estrangement. They helped with practical matters like shopping and transportation to medical appointments. They were available in emergencies, if Ethel had a return of active suicidal thoughts or behavior.

From these two cases we can see two different approaches to the relation between pastoral care and mental health care in a person with non-acute suicidal ideas. We want to highlight the significant role of the congregation and the congregation's leader (pastor, priest or rabbi) with the non-acute suicidal person. The parish can be the center of education about suicide for its members. It can be a resource for suicide prevention, for helping actively and potentially suicidal members get the referrals and help that they need. The congregation is often a network of friendships among members who can be sensitive to the early signs that a friend needs help. Congregations provide support for persons recovering from attempted suicide and for persons with chronic suicidal ideas and behavior, such as Ethel. The congregation may also play an important role in the recovery of family members and friends of someone who successfully commits suicide. The multiple caring relationships that develop over the years among members of a congregation who have passed through many of life's milestones together form a strong network of support that can be important in education, prevention, and support related to suicide.

VI. The relation between pastoral and mental health care in acute suicidal cases

As we have already noted, the relation between pastoral care and mental health care of suicidal persons seems to take on a very different quality when we are dealing with persons with active or acute suicidal ideas or behavior, like James or Ethel at the times when she was actively suicidal. We will review three positions regarding the relation of pastoral care and mental health care in these cases. The positions are that suicidality is a spiritual problem, that acute suicidality is a mental health problem, and that acute suicidality is both a spiritual and mental health problem.

Suicide as a spiritual problem. It may be a common response among lay people, mental health professionals, and clergy as well to think of suicidal behavior as a sign of severe mental illness, in which spiritual issues are absent or minimally involved. Thus to think of suicide as a spiritual problem in which pastoral care may play a role requires some defense. In their article, "Should Clergy Counsel Suicidal Persons?," Sullender and Malony offer such an argument (1990).

They write, "We would like to argue that suicide is primarily, although not entirely, a spiritual problem." They argue that in suicide the issues of meaning and purpose in life, of hope, of worth and of renewal of life are central and that these are essentially religious issues.

Our three cases seem, to some extent, to support this argument. As we have noted, the themes of estrangement, abandonment, betrayal, isolation, and conflicted relations with significant others including God and church, seem to run through each case. In each case we also see efforts to overcome this estrangement, efforts to search for wholeness through pastoral counseling and/or pastoral care. When the pain of conflict or abandonment was most acute, suicidal thinking and behavior seemed to increase in all three cases.

If suicide is, at least in part, a spiritual problem, what are the implications for the relation between pastoral care and mental health care? The first implication is that mental health care which is not attentive to the spiritual aspect of suicidal persons is not sufficient. Mental health professionals working with suicidal persons cannot ignore the spiritual aspect of the problem, and pastoral care providers cannot simply refer these cases and forget about them.

The second implication is that pastoral care must be provided in order to address the spiritual aspects of suicide. Sullender and Malony (1990) state that "Clergy from differing religious traditions have differing ways of understanding suicide and the nature of the helping relationship." But regardless of these differences, "What suicidal persons really need to hear and experience anew is the 'good news' of God's forgiveness and new life. The news needs to be good, not bad. Moreover, suicidal parishioners need to *experience* it in a deep and personal way, not just hear it proclaimed again" (Sullender & Malony, 1990).

Some might argue that suicide is primarily a spiritual problem and what is needed is primarily spiritual care, such as the experienced good news referred to above. We prefer the position that suicide has a spiritual aspect which must be taken into consideration along with other mental health aspects and that effective care must be multi-disciplinary. This is similar to the position taken by

Sullender and Malony (1990): "We would argue that suicide and suicide-threatening depression must be understood holistically."

Suicide as a mental health problem. In contrast to the position just discussed, some argue that suicide is essentially a symptom of mental illness. Thus, while suicide may result from loss of meaning, despair, demoralization, or other affects identified as religious or spiritual, suicide and suicidal ideation are also symptoms of severe depression. In the past few years we have come to recognize that alcoholism is a disease. We are required to see it as such in order to effect any real change. Similarly, suicide or suicidal potential is a symptom of severe mental illness which requires mental health care, a severe illness which blocks addressing the spiritual issues in any meaningful way and which must be addressed as such before the spiritual care can take place.

In our case material James may provide the most dramatic illustration of this perspective. James seemed so caught up in his rage, and his potential to harm Mary, others, or himself was so great, that he was unable to hear or participate in any good news. His mental illness overshadowed the spiritual aspects of his problem and precluded pastoral or spiritual care.

What are the implications of this view for the pastoral caregiver's work? The view that suicidal behavior is symptomatic of a severe mental illness dictates that pastoral caregivers make an appropriate referral for any person who shows signs of this illness. It is like making a referral for someone who appears to be having a heart attack. Emergency medical care must be obtained.

It could be argued that efforts to help James when he was most violent and self-destructive were not simply efforts to address his mental illness. For example, it could be said that as the pastoral counselor paid more attention to James' mental illness, the counselor was providing good pastoral care for both James and Mary. Or it could be said that the pastoral intervention that was most needed in this relationship was to help to move James and Mary apart so that the destructive pattern could be arrested and James could get the help he needed. We find some sympathy with these views, but we prefer to make a distinction here which focuses clear attention on acute suicidal behavior as a symptom of serious mental illness which requires appropriate medical attention.

The pastor's work with Ethel illustrates another way in which pastoral care is related to mental health care for acutely suicidal persons. Prior to her second and third hospitalizations, when her suicidal thoughts and behavior became more predominant, she called her pastor as did some friends from the congregation who were alarmed. The pastor came to her home and in consultation with Ethel, her family, her psychiatrist and the hospital chaplain, the pastor worked with Ethel to help her see the need for hospitalization. The pastor also developed a plan to keep her safe until hospitalization was possible, and then drove her to the hospital.

While she was hospitalized the pastor visited her regularly, brought her the Sunday bulletin, kept her informed about her friends in the congregation, talked with her, and prayed with her. As someone who knew the local community well, the pastor was also a resource to Ethel and the health care team in finding resources for follow-up outpatient family counseling.

The pastor's work with Ethel at these times could be seen as similar to pastoral care that might occur with a member of the congregation who had fallen and broken a hip. The primary illness here was not seen as spiritual, but supportive pastoral care was an important aspect of the total care provided to Ethel.

As we consider the view that suicide is a mental illness, we also want to mention two special obligations which clergy face in the case of suicide and which they rarely face in other situations: the seal of the confessional and the legal obligation to inform. In cases of serious potential for self-harm, the seal of the confessional may be broken. Similarly, in these cases, the special privileges of confidentiality for clergy do not remove them from the legal obligation to inform family about the client's suicide potential [*Editor's note: The legal obligations for clergy in this situation vary from state to state, so clergy should be aware of the laws governing the state in which they minister*]. Both of these obligations seem to reinforce the view that acute suicide potential cannot be treated like a normal spiritual problem.

In regard to the issue of the obligation to inform, the context for ministry is again important to consider. Pastoral counselors working in pastoral counseling centers and pastors working with persons who are not members of their congregations must function like other mental health professionals and make appropriate referrals for suicidal persons. They are under a legal obligation to inform. Pastors in local congregations working with members of their congregation should make such referrals, but may not be held to the same legal obligation to do so (Sullender & Malony, 1990).

Suicide as a spiritual problem *and* mental illness. As we noted earlier, we think it best to view acute suicidality as a problem with both spiritual and mental health dimensions. The balance of attention given to either dimension and the goals for counseling may shift from time to time. For example, the pastoral counselor working with James and Mary felt that when the destructive forces of suicide made themselves present, it was necessary to change the assessment of the case and the treatment plan.

In the case of Ethel, tandem care — the provision of both pastoral care and mental health care — took place both during some periods when she did not evidence any suicidal behavior and when she was acutely suicidal and hospitalized.

During her hospitalizations both her psychiatrist and the chaplain saw her on a daily basis. The psychiatrist provided medication to help with her depression and anxiety. He observed her suicidal symptoms and wrote orders for her participation in the milieu of the treatment unit. He supported the social worker's work with Ethel and her family and the chaplain's involvement in her care.

The chaplain saw Ethel to provide support, to discuss her feelings that her life was empty and mattered to no one. He also provided a forum in which she could discuss her feelings about why God seemed so far away from her and was not listening to her prayers, and to help her reach out to God again to share her concerns with God in prayer. The chaplain interpreted and supported the treatment recommendations of the staff when Ethel was anxious or resisting them. The chaplain made recommendations to Ethel and the care team for Ethel's post-discharge care and activity. Some of those recommendations focused on Ethel's low sense of self-worth and reluctance to be involved in activities which interested her and enhanced her sense of worth. The chaplain also served as a liaison with the pastor, helping him participate in Ethel's care and discharge planning.

In viewing suicide as a problem with both spiritual and mental health aspects, we reject the view that pastors only work with cases where there is little or only mild mental illness and must refer all cases of serious mental illness to other mental health practitioners. We prefer the model of tandem care, where the client receives care from both a pastor or pastoral counselor and a mental health professional, with the balance and focus of care being adjusted between these professionals as the dynamics of the case dictate (Holinger, 1985).

VII. The client's role in distinguishing between pastoral and mental health care

Up to this point we have discussed the relation between pastoral and mental health care for suicidal persons but we have ignored a key perspective, the client's. What role can and should the client play in establishing the relation between pastoral care and mental health care in their own individual care?

The leaders of local congregations — pastors, priests and rabbis — are perhaps more aware than most of the role that congregation members will play in determining the relation between pastoral care and mental health care. We have heard many stories about situations in which the priest or rabbi saw signs of serious mental illness in a member of their congregation who refused to be referred to a mental health professional.

What is the pastor or rabbi to do in such a situation? Is it best to provide some pastoral care because a little care is better than none? It may make the difference between life and death, and it may build a bridge which will enable the referral to be accepted at a later date. Or is it better to refuse to provide any care unless the referral is accepted, arguing that a lack of competence, not to mention time, may mean the care provided could do more harm than good?

There are obviously no easy answers to these questions. It is possible to refuse to provide pastoral care unless a mental health referral is accepted. This might underscore the seriousness with which the referral is viewed, but it does run the risk that no help will be provided and the congregant will be alienated from one possible key source of help, the congregation leader. Another option would be to proceed to provide what counsel one is capable of providing with a view toward continued efforts to make a referral to a mental health professional. In such cases it would be imperative for the pastor or rabbi to be in consultation with a competent and knowledgeable mental health professional who can assist with the assessment of the case and think through the treatment and intervention options with the pastor, priest, or rabbi.

We had a conversation with a pastor who we think handles situations like this creatively. He tells members of his congregation who come to him for counsel, "I'm not a psychologist. I'm not a psychiatrist. I'm not a social worker with an MSW degree. I am a pastor. I will give you the best counsel I can. But it will not be psychology and it will not be psychiatry." This introductory comment establishes a sense of limits in the pastoral care. When this pastor feels that the parishioner needs more help than he can offer, or that some psychiatric help is needed in addition to what he can offer, he says, "Look, I think this is a psychiatric issue. I don't drill teeth, I don't fix glasses, and I don't do psychiatry." The pastor reports that his approach has worked well for him and that it helps the members of his congregation accept mental health care and still feel good about themselves. We also like the way in which it allows for the continuation of tandem care where that seems appropriate.

In our case material, Ethel was very active in shaping the roles of those who were working with her. She preferred to call her pastor or the hospital chaplain rather than her psychiatrist. She took an active part in defining the relation between pastoral and mental health perspectives in her care. She preferred the pastoral to the psychiatric perspective. It appears to have less stigma attached to it for her. If there is a boundary between pastoral and mental health care in suicidal persons (or others), it may be that by the choices they make and the preferences they express our clients play an important role in defining that boundary.

Ethel had professional contact with a large number of pastoral and mental health workers. The medical and mental health professionals included her internist, her psychiatrist, her inpatient nurse with whom she was very close, the social worker on the psychiatric unit, and an outpatient family therapist. The pastoral care professionals she worked with included a pastoral counselor in a community pastoral counseling center, her pastor, and the hospital chaplain. Ethel was active in defining her relationship with all of these professional people. She respected each of them as professionals, but she also wanted to have a personal relationship with each of them. She brought them all gifts. She wanted to know about their families. She wanted to know how they were all doing. She had a wonderful way of personalizing all those relationships. At times Ethel was explicit in saying that she did not want to be seen as a person with emotional problems, and she hated to have to go for help for her problems. Thus, she chose to constitute all her professional relationships as personal friendships.

This was true of her relationship with the hospital chaplain. When the content of the chaplain's conversations with Ethel is examined, it is more like the conversation between friends than between a professional caregiver and a client. The chaplain expressed interest in Ethel as a person. The chaplain reminded her of things that were good for her, that she should take care of herself, that she should treat herself well, and that she should not hurt herself. He was also an advocate for Ethel within the hospital system, particularly when outpatient consultations were not working out correctly. At those times and at a few others, he did some problem solving with and for Ethel. The chaplain and Ethel did not discuss religious topics often. We might say that this was a relationship in which the pastoral aspect of the relationship was implicitly understood but not explicitly discussed.

VIII. Conclusion

We view suicide as a symptom of both severe mental illness and profound spiritual suffering. Thus we feel that the perspectives of both pastoral care and mental health care are needed to understand and treat suicidal persons. In cases where suicidal ideation and behavior are non-acute, pastoral care, particularly as expressed in the work of specialized pastoral counselors, is able to address both dimensions of the suicidal person's need. In cases where suicidal ideation and behavior are actively present, tandem care — both pastoral care and mental health care — is needed. The particular form, proportions, and relationship of each type of care to the other will vary depending on the circumstances of each case. In all cases of ministry with suicidal persons, pastoral care providers need both competence and consultation.

Further, our three cases suggest to us that pastoral care professionals and mental health professionals alike need to be sensitive to the suicidal client's search for relatedness, belonging, and community. As we previously noted, Sullender and Malony (1990) believe that what the suicidal person needs most of all is "to experience the good news in a deep and personal way." The pastoral counselor working with Jane captured the significance of this dynamic, reflecting, "Suicide may be understood as the act that comes from feeling utterly abandoned. I believe Jane will never commit suicide because she is finding people who are not abandoning her and she is abandoning herself less and less. I also believe that in the future she will find security in God."

References

Holinger P: *Pastoral Care of Severe Emotional Disorders*. New York, Irvington Publishers, Inc., 1985.
Sullender RS, Malony HN: Should clergy counsel suicidal persons? *Journal of Pastoral Care* 44: 203-211, 1990.

Chapter 15

Suicidal Thoughts:
Spiritual Issue or Mental Illness?

Paul C. Holinger, M.D.

The topic of this section is actually a question: Do suicidal thoughts reflect a spiritual and philosophical issue, or an aspect of mental illness? Needless to say, this is an extremely complex theoretical and clinical topic. In one sense, of course, the answer depends on the nature and context of the suicidal thoughts. Such thoughts may be spiritual, or evidence of serious mental problems, or both. But I would like to address this topic briefly from a very clinical and practical point of view. It seems that our topic is, really, an implied question: How does one determine whether or not suicidal thoughts are spiritual issues or evidence of mental illness? I think there is a very definite answer to this question. But first as a way to get to this answer, three clinical vignettes may be useful to consider.

The case of Mrs. Preston

Pastor Josh Manning had been informed by a church school teacher that Cara (age four and a half years) and Lisa (age three years) Preston were upset when they arrived Sunday morning, with their slacks and sweaters on backwards, with scratches on their faces and hands, and not having had any breakfast. This was a drastic departure from the usual. The family had been members of the church for three years. He therefore contacted Mrs. Preston (age 31) and asked if he might visit her at home. She said she would rather see him at his office the next day at 2:15 p.m. sharp.

Mrs. Preston arrived at 2:15 wearing rumpled slacks and blouse, hair moderately disheveled, no makeup on, and very tense facial muscles.

Mrs. Preston: I am on time, Pastor, aren't I? I feel it is so important to be on time — why, it could be so inconsiderate to keep someone waiting and I always tell the girls they should be on time as that is what being good girls is all about. Jesus would say that, don't you think, Pastor? I certainly do.

Pastor: (*Gently interrupting Mrs. Preston and guiding her to a chair in his office*). Thank you for being prompt. How are you?

Mrs. Preston: Well! I have been so busy lately. I was just certain I wouldn't make it on time.

Pastor: Well, you are here now, Mrs. Preston. Why don't we just try to relax and you tell me about all these things you're doing. You know, I contacted you because Cara and Lisa seemed upset on Sunday morning —can you tell me what happened?

Mrs. Preston: Well, we had so much to do I had to get the girls up very early Sunday morning. (*This was her first sentence spoken in a relaxed manner*).

Pastor: How early?

Mrs. Preston: Oh, we got up a little after 5 (a.m.), I think... I think... we had so much to do, you know... (*her voice trailing off, she appeared sad*).

Pastor: Just what did you do?

Mrs. Preston: Well, well we got into the car and went to do all of the errands — (*pause*) — you know! (*anxiety, tense facial muscles*).

Pastor: Now relax. Mrs. Preston, can you tell me just what you needed to do at 5 on Sunday morning?

Mrs. Preston: (*Gets out of her chair and walks about the room: she appears quite distracted; she does not answer*).

Pastor: Could you tell me how Lisa and Cara got those scratches?

Mrs. Preston: (*Still standing*). From the glass — (*voice trailing off*).

Pastor: What glass, Mrs. Preston?

Mrs. Preston: The window, no the windshield...

Pastor: Your car windshield?

Mrs. Preston: Oh yes, the garage door broke the windshield (*sad, quite matter-of-factly*).

Pastor: Mrs. Preston, how did the garage door break the car windshield?

Mrs. Preston: Well, I had to drive through it, and it broke, that's how.

Pastor: You had to drive through the garage door, Mrs. Preston? (*asked calmly*)

Mrs. Preston: Yes, I had to (*voice trailing off again, she abruptly sits, but in another chair*).

Pastor: Tell me about driving through the door.

Mrs. Preston: He told me to!! (*said with real exasperation in her voice*). I wouldn't do such a thing unless I was told to, you know!

Pastor: Who told you?

Mrs. Preston: (*interrupting*) You're not angry? — (*tension in her voice*).

Pastor: No, I am not angry, but I am concerned, as I don't want anything to happen to you or the girls, and driving through the garage door is very dangerous.

Mrs. Preston: I know that! But he told me I had to do it — (*suddenly her voice trailing off*).

Pastor: Who told you? (*very gently and quietly*)

Mrs. Preston: Jesus. He told me He had sacrificed His life for me, and that I should sacrifice mine for Him.

Pastor: How long have you been hearing this?

Mrs. Preston: Well — (*long pause*) — Well, He contacted me on the evening after... I think it was the evening after, maybe it was the morning after... but I think it was the evening after... but I think it was the evening. You're not angry with me?

Pastor: No, I'm not angry.

Mrs. Preston: He contacted me the evening after Dick left for his downstate job. You know he designed the whole new bridge system, and he had to go down there to see about the construction.

Pastor: Have you ever talked with Jesus before?

Mrs. Preston: Yes.

Pastor: Can you tell me when?

Mrs. Preston: Well, I think it was before Cara was born, and He was telling me how to be pregnant.

Pastor: Were you in the hospital then?

Mrs. Preston (*interrupting*): I don't want to!! (*angrily*)

Pastor: You don't want to what, Mrs. Preston?

Mrs. Preston: I don't want to go back there.

Pastor: Where?

Mrs. Preston: Apple Creek State!! It's horrid, nasty, ugly, and Jesus hated it and they were mean and I won't go!! (*still angry*).

Pastor: Apple Creek Hospital is near Pleasantville, isn't it? (*She nods assent*). Mrs. Preston, that's over 200 miles from here, and of course you won't go there. But it is important for you to get help as soon as possible as we cannot have these voices telling you to do things — especially things that are dangerous to you and your daughters. I know Dr. Foster, an excellent psychiatrist and he is on staff at Ridgeview, a fine hospital. He is good and very kind. He won't be angry with you.

Mrs. Preston: (*Long silence*) I don't like the voices... or only sometimes (*said with sadness*).

Pastor: I don't understand.

Mrs. Preston: I don't like them when they tell me to hurt my girls. I didn't do it you know, the time before. I had to go through the garage door. I didn't do what they said so they punished me and I didn't want to — (*voice trailing, long pause*). I don't want Cara and Lisa hurt. Reverend Manning, I don't, I don't (*said slowly and sadly*) (Holinger, 1985, pp. 113-115).

The case of someone struggling with despair and suicide

Let me now present you something written by someone who was struggling with issues of despair and suicide:

"But, as was pointed out above, the degree of consciousness potentiates despair. In the same degree that a man has a truer conception of despair while still remaining in it, and in the same degree that he is more conscious of being in despair, in that same degree is his despair more intense. He who, with the consciousness that suicide is despair, and to that extent with the true conception of what despair is, then commits suicide — that man has a more intense despair than the man who commits suicide without having the true conception that suicide is despair; conversely, the less true his conception of suicide is, the less intense his despair" (Bretall, 1946, pp. 350-351).

The case of a royal family member

Let me now share part of an evaluation of a 22-year-old man, a member of the Royal Family of one of the Scandinavian countries.

Patient: I am not sure whether I want to live or not. I don't know whether it's more courageous to put up with the hassles in my everyday life, or to fight these troubles by just ending it all. Dying is just like sleeping — and with that kind of sleep, if I can end all my problems, then I'm all for it! So if death is like sleep.... but when you're sleeping, you dream, and I guess that's the dilemma for me.

Therapist: Can you elaborate on that?

Patient: Well, if death is like sleep, and you dream during sleep, what happens when you're dead? That sure makes me think twice. I mean, I think about it, Doc... Who would put up with all the craziness of life, the unfairness, the heartbreaks...? Why tolerate all the toils and troubles of a weary life — except for the dread of what happens *after* death! We put up with life because nobody has ever returned from the dead, and we don't know what awaits us there. So thinking about *that* makes us a little afraid to jump in. And so, just when I'm resolved to end it, I start thinking about it all, and just don't take any action on it.

Discussion

Here we have three vignettes that address our topic in one form or another. The first vignette was an actual transcript of a pastor and his parishioner; the second came from *Sickness Unto Death* by Søren Kierkegaard (Kierkegaard wrote that passage in 1849); and the third vignette can easily be recognized as a paraphrasing of our Danish friend, Hamlet, whose famous "To be or not to be" soliloquy I transposed into a clinical interview.

In terms of viewing our topic as a clinical question of whether suicidal thoughts represent mental illness or a spiritual issue, I think these vignettes beg this very important question. I think there is a clinical and very practical answer — and that is the mental status examination within the context of our empathic understanding of the patient. The mental status exam is the one way we have of ascertaining in the clinical situation whether or not a person's suicidal thoughts and preoccupations are evidence of a spiritual issue or mental illness. Any good general psychiatry textbook (easily obtainable at a local bookstore or medical school library) will have extensive and valuable information about the mental status exam (see also Holinger, 1985). Let us briefly review some of the fundamental aspects of the mental status exam. For example:

Orientation — is the person oriented to time, place, and person? If not, an organic brain syndrome or severe agitated depression are among the possibilities.

Affect — is the person sad, agitated, depressed, anxious, or showing little affect?

Memory — is memory, both short- and long-term, normal or impaired?

Insight — how much insight does the person have about his/her own situation?

Hallucinations — is the person seeing or hearing voices which are not really there? If so, is he/she following directions issued by the voices? If so, it is likely that a psychiatric emergency exists.

Delusion — a fixed false belief which is not consistent with a person's upbringing and culture. Of all people, the clergyperson may be the most able to assess whether or not a person's religious thoughts and feelings represent something psychologically unusual or not.

Suicidal thoughts — we have to remind ourselves that if we have any suspicion that a person may be suicidal, we need to ask him/her directly about those thoughts and feelings, and if they have a plan, etc. Our asking about suicide will never be enough to *push* someone to suicide, but it may be enough to *keep* someone from suicide.

To return to the vignettes:

Of course, without an actual clinical interview, no reliable assessment of the spiritual-or-mental illness and suicidality issues can be made — and only the vignette with Mrs. Preston provides such extensive clinical information. However, some assessment of the other two vignettes can be attempted as well. First, Mrs. Preston's issues clearly fall on the side of mental illness, albeit within a spiritual context. She is, in fact, quite psychotic: she is hallucinating, agitated, shows little insight into her condition, and is suicidal (the voices are telling her to sacrifice herself). In short, she is a very real danger to herself and her children, and the pastor is confronted with a serious psychiatric emergency. At the moment, one doesn't know the cause of the psychosis, and a number of possibilities exist: for example, severe agitated depression, manic phase of bipolar disorder, psychotic episode in a schizophrenic, or medical illness such as a brain tumor, untreated diabetes, other endocrine disorder, or a drug reaction.

By contrast, Kierkegaard's writing appears to fall more into the spiritual-philosophical realm. Although Kierkegaard may have been depressed, one would certainly need more clinical information and more convincing mental status evidence to justify this as a mental illness problem.

The issues presented in the third case are even more complex. *Hamlet* has spawned a large psychiatric literature, with diagnostic opinions ranging from a garden-variety Oedipal neurosis, to overt psychosis, to feigning of mental illness. In the vignette presented here, the patient clearly seems to be manifesting acute suicidal ideation, with not much more than a bit of obsessiveness to dissuade him from suicide — hence one would probably consider this more of a mental illness than a spiritual issue.

Conclusion

I have briefly addressed the issue of suicidal thoughts as a spiritual issue or mental illness. I have suggested that there is an implied clinical question at stake here and presented three vignettes to highlight different aspects of this question. Finally, I suggested that there is an answer to this clinical question in the form of the mental status examination. The mental status exam is a very powerful tool for us, whether in the pastorate or in the consulting room.

References

Bretall, R (editor): *A Kierkegaard Anthology*. New York, Random House, 1946.

Holinger, PC: *Pastoral Care of Severe Emotional Disorders*. New York, Irvington, 1985.

VII. Appendices: Basic Information about Suicide

Introduction

In Appendix A, Dr. Clark describes the scope of the problem and demographic patterns of suicide in the U.S. with the help of a series of figures. After a brief discussion of the most common methods employed for suicide, he summarizes clinical knowledge about how to recognize persons likely to try suicide and reviews important considerations to keep in mind when trying to connect a suicidal person with mental health services.

Two valuable public reports addressing the problems of suicide contagion and suicide clusters are also reprinted below. In the wake of a cluster of youth suicides in New Jersey in 1988, the Centers for Disease Control convened a group of experts to review public health experiences with suicide clusters and prepare a report entitled "Recommendations for a Community Plan for the Prevention and Containment of Suicide Clusters," which appears here as Appendix B. In 1991, the Association of State and Territorial Health Officials and the New Jersey Department of Health convened a group of experts to prepare another report entitled "Recommendations on Suicide Contagion and the Reporting of Suicide," which appears here as Appendix C.

These reports summarize what is known about the nature and extent of the problems of suicide contagion and suicide clusters. Appendix B includes a series of recommendations about how communities should organize their responses to a series of suicides, or to traumatic deaths which might influence others to attempt suicide, in order to minimize further suicides and minimize sensationalism. This report emphasizes the need for a well-coordinated and directed division of labor among all local service agencies and mental health professionals.

Appendix C cautions that news reports and media sensational-ism may inadvertently encourage further suicide. The report pro-vides guidelines for encouraging responsible media coverage. In particular, it is important to remember that providing specific details on how the suicide occurred may be harmful. Most news reports of suicides should be handled in the way that all other obituaries are routinely handled. Media "investigations" of sui-cide cases — which appear in the form of premature, simplistic speculations — generally have little educational, scientific, or news value.

Appendix A

The Nature of Suicide Risk

David C. Clark, Ph.D.

Mental health professionals customarily distinguish between suicide, suicide attempts, and suicidal thoughts. *Suicide* refers to death by suicide (e.g., a person who dies by self-inflicted gunshot wound or hanging). *Suicide attempt* refers to intentional but non-fatal self-injury (e.g., a person who swallows a lot of pills or cuts his/her wrist, but survives). *Suicidal thought* refers to ideas about killing oneself — fleeting or persistent thoughts — that are not translated into action. It is important to distinguish among these categories because the characteristics of persons in each group tend to be more different than alike.

Thinking a lot about suicide, or preoccupations with the idea of suicide, is not normal or common. Neither is it rare. Suicidal thoughts expressed by a member of a congregation, a friend, a family member, or another clergyperson always warrant concern and a professional evaluation. But in course of daily life in the community, suicidal communications are rarely treated as a cause for serious concern. Most people are surprised when a family member dies by suicide, even though studies indicate that most suicide victims voiced their suicidal ideas or intentions beforehand. Eighty-six percent of parents are not aware when their own offspring develop recurrent suicidal thoughts (Kashani et al., 1989). Sixty-two percent of parents are not aware when their own offspring have *attempted* suicide (Walker et al., 1990). The suicide attempts recognized by parents are not necessarily more severe than the ones not recognized.

Why are suicidal communications and suicidal behavior over-looked so often? Beyond a general reluctance to consult mental health professionals and general anxiety about the cost of professional care, there is another formidable barrier that prevents suicidal persons from being recognized and from receiving the benefit of prompt professional attention — the common tendency for others to respond to suicidal communications with *disbelief*.

Faced with a loved one who voices suicidal thoughts, most people decide that the suicidal thoughts reflect nothing more than: (a) exasperation; (b) a hollow threat; (c) a cry for help that does not necessarily presage suicidal behavior; or (d) an innocent joke. The elements of anguish, despair, and neediness inherent to a suicidal communication are so intense and burdensome that sensitive and loving people — even spouses, parents, and pastors — often respond to suicidal communications with an unmeditated reflex of denial or minimization, as in: "She can't really mean it," "He isn't serious," or "She isn't the kind of person who would actually do harm to herself." These kinds of responses generally shield the hearer from understanding that something is profoundly wrong. The bottom line is that clergyperson should **always assume talk about death and/or suicide is serious and cause for deep concern, regardless of the context, until proven otherwise**.

The scope of the problem

Suicide is the eighth leading cause of death in the United States (Table 1). More than thirty thousand persons die by suicide each year. One and a half percent of all deaths are suicides. These facts should make it clear that suicide is a *major public health problem* and not a narrowly-defined psychological or psychiatric issue. When the leading causes of death are ranked according to how many years of life are lost before the age of 65, suicide rises to become the fourth leading cause of "years of premature life lost." Suicide is an equal-opportunity tragedy that touches every age group, ethnic group, race, and level of income or education. U.S. suicide rates fall in the middle of the pack when compared to those for all other countries.

Table 1
10 Leading Causes of Death in the U.S., 1990

Table 1			
10 Leading Causes of Death in the U.S., 1990			
Rank	Cause of death	Annual rate / 100,000	No. of deaths
1	Diseases of the heart	289.5	720,058
2	Malignant neoplasms	203.2	505,322
3	Cerebrovascular diseases	57.9	144,088
4	Accidents	37.0	91,983
5	Chronic obstructive pulmonary diseases	34.9	86,679
6	Pneumonia & influenza	32.0	79,513
7	Diabetes mellitus	19.2	47,664
8	SUICIDE	12.4	30,906
9	Chronic liver disease & cirrhosis	10.4	25,815
10	HIV infection	10.1	25,188
—	All other causes	157.3	391,247

Turning our attention to non-fatal suicidal behavior, national survey data show that 2.9% of living adults have tried to kill themselves before, 0.3% have made a suicide attempt during the most recent year, and nine percent admit to having had suicidal thoughts in the past year (Moscicki et al., 1988; Petronis et al., 1990). Considered together, the fatal and non-fatal suicidal actions of a family member profoundly alter the lives of more than 3,800,000 Americans each year.

Sex and race differences

For reasons that remain unexplained, the suicide rate for males is four times higher than the suicide rate for females, and the suicide rate for whites is two times higher than that for blacks or Hispanics (Figure 1). When these *rate* differences are applied to the current demographics of the U.S., they make for lopsided trends in the actual *numbers* of suicides. Seventy-three percent of all suicides involve white males, 18% white females, seven percent non-white males, and two percent non-white females (Figure 2).

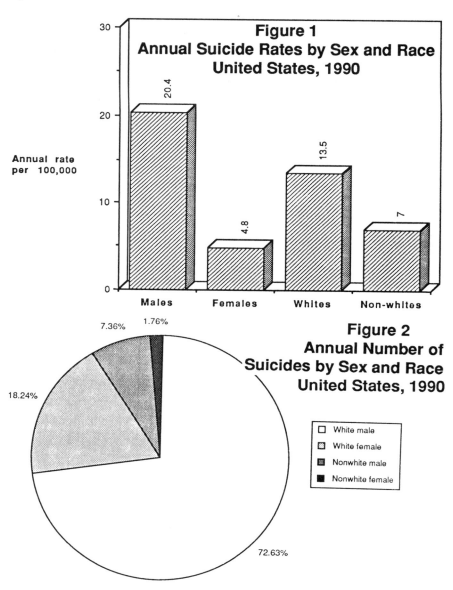

Figure 1
Annual Suicide Rates by Sex and Race
United States, 1990

Annual rate per 100,000

Figure 2
Annual Number of
Suicides by Sex and Race
United States, 1990

☐ White male
▨ White female
▩ Nonwhite male
■ Nonwhite female

The high rate of suicide among white males should not divert our attention from the terrible cost in life of suicide among females, blacks, Hispanics, Asians, and other minority groups. Certain specific (not all) groups or tribes of Native Americans are associated with suicide rates higher than seen elsewhere in North America. Yet it remains true that: (a) white males are at greater risk for death by suicide than females or non-whites; (b) the pre-dominance of white male suicides means that national statistics describe white male suicide patterns better than they describe female or non-white suicide patterns; and (c) the race/ethnicity differences noted are not consistent with any simple "psychoso-cial stress" model of suicide, since it is impossible to argue that blacks or Hispanics are (as groups) under less social or economic pressure in the United States than whites.

Turning our attention to persons who make non-fatal suicide attempts, we find a very different pattern applies. Suicide attempters are three times more likely to be female than male. The suicide attempt rates for whites, African-Americans, and Hispanics are very similar.

Age differences: Death by suicide

Those under age 25 years make up 15% of the U.S. population and account for 16% of all suicides. Those aged 65 years and over make up 12% of the population but account for 21% of all sui-cides. At this point in history, men aged 65 years and over are associated with the highest rate of death by suicide (Figure 3).

But U.S. suicide rates are not uniformly higher for all elderly persons. Middle-aged women have much lower suicide rates than middle-aged men, and the rate of suicide for women *declines* after age 65 (Figure 3). Middle-aged non-whites have much lower sui-cide rates than whites, and the rate of suicide for non-whites *does not increase appreciably* after age 65 (Figure 4). Only white males show a steep increase in suicide rates after age 65.

Since 73% of all suicides involve white males, and since the white male suicide rate is highest for those aged 65 years and over, it would be logical to conclude that the bulk of all suicides implicate elderly white males — but this is a false conclusion. Thirty-nine percent of all suicides involve persons between the ages of 25 and 44 (Figure 5) because the elderly account for a relatively small fraction of the total population (12%), and because those in the "baby-boom" generation (ages 39 to 48) account for such a large fraction of the total population at this point in time. The "typical" case of suicide involves a married man in his 30s who leaves behind a wife and children.

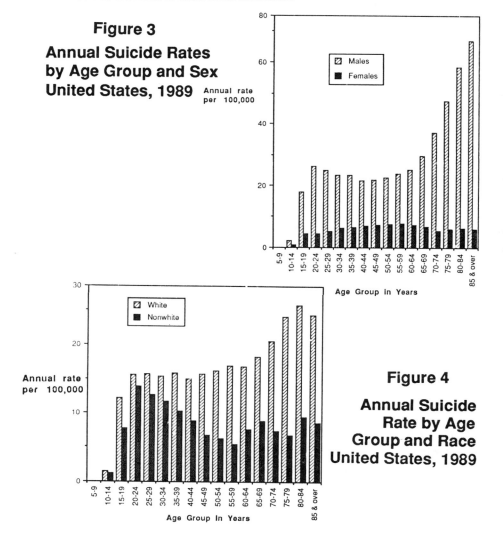

Figure 3

Annual Suicide Rates by Age Group and Sex United States, 1989

Annual rate per 100,000

Figure 4

Annual Suicide Rate by Age Group and Race United States, 1989

Figure 5
Number of Suicides by Age
United States, 1989

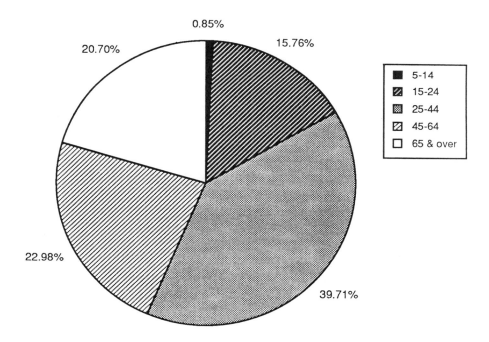

Figure 6 illustrates the changing suicide rates from 1933 to 1990 for all persons, for persons 15 to 24 years old, and for persons 65 years and over. The general population suicide rate was highest during the Great Depression of the 1930s, dropped during World War II, and has been fairly stable since 1945 — actually increasing slowly since 1945.

Figure 6
Annual Suicide Rates by Age
United States, 1933-1990

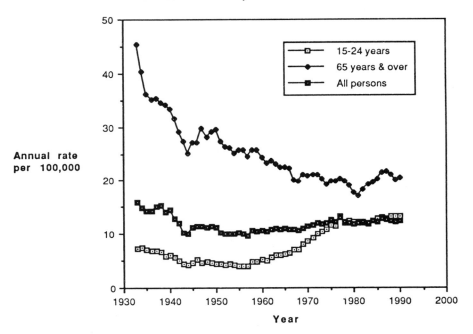

Annual rate per 100,000

15-24 years
65 years & over
All persons

Year

Although the U.S. suicide rate has not changed much during the past 50 years, the suicide rates for specific age groups have changed enormously. The suicide rate for persons 65 years and over was almost three times *higher* in 1933 than in 1981 — the suicide rate for elderly persons declined steadily between 1933 and 1981, rose 23% between 1981 and 1986, then dropped again. The suicide rate for young persons was three times lower in 1955 than in 1977 — the suicide rate for the young rose steadily between 1955 and 1977, and has remained relatively stable between 1977 and 1990. While there are many theories about why elderly suicide rates have dropped so steeply and youth rates have climbed so steeply during the last 60 years, none of these theories have succeeded in generating accurate predictions about future suicide trends for a particular age group.

The trend line for the elderly suicide rate bears watching. A large percentage of the U.S. population is concentrated in the post-war "baby boom" generation. If older adult suicide rates should begin to rise between now and the year 2010, when the "boomers" begin to reach the age of 65, rising suicide rates and a large population bulge in the elderly age bracket could combine to yield an unprecedented number of suicides.

Age differences: Suicide attempts

Once again, the trends for persons who have made non-fatal suicide attempts are a little different. Considering adults aged 18 years and over, national survey data shows that those between the ages of 25 and 44 are the most likely to report a history of having made suicide attempts (4%), followed by those 18 to 24 years (3.4%), 45 to 65 years (2.1%), and those aged 65 years and over (only 1.1%) (Moscicki et al., 1988). One important implication of the different age patterns associated with suicide and attempted suicide is that while the elderly are less likely to attempt suicide, death is more likely to result.

High-school-aged students are more likely to report suicidal ideas and behavior than adults. A recent national survey by the Centers for Disease Control (1991) suggested that 27% of all high school students report "they have thought seriously about attempting suicide." Only 16% of the same students report making "a specific plan to attempt suicide," however, and fewer yet (8%) report they "actually attempted suicide." In another large study of college freshmen, Meehan and colleagues (1992) found that over the course of their lifetimes, ten percent had attempted to take their own life, five percent had suffered injury due to an attempt, and three percent had sought medical care due to an attempt. In the most recent 12 months, two percent had attempted to take their own life, one percent had suffered injury due to an attempt and 0.4% had sought medical care due to an attempt.

Family situation

It is often said that suicide rates are lower for the married and higher for the separated, widowed, or divorced. In fact the presence or absence of responsibility for children appears to influence suicide risk more directly than marital status. Men and women with responsibility for children are statistically less likely to die by suicide. When a man or woman with children does succumb to suicide, it sometimes happens that the suicide victim kills the children first in a combination homicide-suicide.

The immediate families of persons who die by suicide fit no simple stereotype. At the time of death, for example, most adolescent suicide victims were living with both their biological parents, and most elderly suicide victims enjoyed strong social and family ties.

As already discussed, the "typical" suicide victim is a white male between the ages of 25 and 44 years — often a man who leaves behind a widow and small children. While a number of support groups for the adult family members of suicide victims have cropped up all across the U.S. during the last twenty years, there are still few groups or professional services designed for the surviving children. These children's lives are disrupted by the loss of one parent, acute grief in the other parent, economic and geographic dislocation, and the stigma unique to suicide. It is often difficult for a widow in this situation to locate professional services for her children — but the children's needs are often acute. Pioneering groups for suicide survivors in Chicago and Piscataway, New Jersey offer separate groups for mothers and their children. The two groups meet at the same time in close proximity to one another. We hope these types of groups become more widely available.

The relationship between non-fatal suicide attempts and marital status is more faithful to popular stereotype. Persons who are separated or divorced are four times more likely to make attempts than those who are married, single, or widowed.

Employment status

In the U.S., there is no strong or direct relationship between rates of unemployment or poverty and regional suicide rates. Most adults who die by suicide were employed at the time of death.

The impact of unemployment on non-fatal suicide attempt behavior seems to be a little more direct. Persons who make suicide attempts are one and a half times more likely to be unemployed than persons who do not make attempts. Regional suicide attempt rates may rise during times of rising unemployment, but attempt rates reach a ceiling at levels of *moderate* unemployment. Further increases in unemployment do not translate directly into more suicide attempts.

Methods

Sixty percent of all deaths by suicide are due to gunshot wounds, most to the head or chest. Hanging is the second most common method of suicide, accounting for 14% of all cases. Suicide by gun is the leading method of suicide for *both* men and women (Figure 7). In fact, forty-seven percent of all deaths by firearms in the United States each year are attributable to suicide. Both handguns and long guns are used to commit suicide. There is evidence that the presence of a gun in the household is a risk factor for adolescent suicide, regardless of whether or not: (a) family members have been trained about gun safety, (b) the gun is stored under lock and key, or (c) the gun is stored without ammunition (Brent et al., 1991).

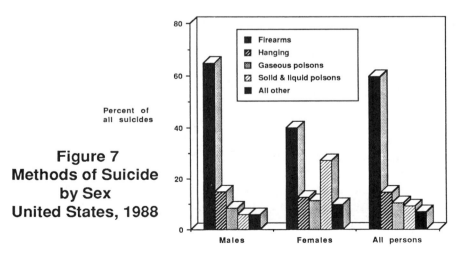

**Figure 7
Methods of Suicide
by Sex
United States, 1988**

Since most suicides occur in the home, family members are usually the first to discover the victim. The shock of unexpectedly discovering a loved one dead by violence in the familiar setting of one's own home is usually a traumatic experience that leaves its own unique stamp on grief. The element of surprise, the gruesome circumstances of the death scene, and the obligation to respond to an emergency (e.g., by cutting down the hanging victim, by summoning police or ambulance) often impose an extraordinary strain on the first persons arriving on the scene. Family members and friends who witness a suicide or who stumble onto the aftermath of suicide without any advance warning should be routinely referred for psychological evaluation. In the absence of professional help, a post-traumatic stress disorder may cripple their ability to grieve and/or function during the ensuing months or years.

Persons who make non-fatal suicide attempts tend to use different methods than the ones used by persons who die by suicide. Seventy percent of attempts involve poisoning or drug overdose. Another 22 percent involve cutting or slashing. Some attempts result in no or minimal physical injury. Other attempts have serious medical consequences, as when the person becomes comatose or loses large amounts of blood. It is generally a mistake to evaluate a suicide attempt solely in terms of its medical consequences.

Every suicide attempt, however trivial or deadly in appearance, represents a mix of motives, including both a wish to live and a wish to die. In cases where the wish to live is stronger (e.g., persons who scratch their wrist superficially with a razor), it is tempting to view the attempt as non-dangerous — i.e., simply a "cry for help" or an "attention-getting maneuver." Stereotyped interpretations such as these interfere with the task of evaluating the (often subtle) countervailing wish to die. The simple truth is: (a) some people kill themselves hours, days, or weeks after a very innocuous attempt, and (b) some people who just explained that they did not really intend to kill themselves in a first suicide attempt go on to kill themselves shortly thereafter.

One should avoid falling into the trap of thinking that since a person has not attempted suicide before, the chances are low that he/she will make a serious attempt in the future. People who have been treated for non-fatal suicide attempts before are five times more likely to die by suicide than other people. But it is also true that half of all persons who die by suicide have never made any suicide attempts before — have never made any attempts that might serve as a clue to their capacity for suicide (Clark & Horton-Deutsch, 1992).

Recognizing someone at risk for suicide

Thoughts about death that last more than a few days, thoughts about suicide that last more than a day, or preoccupation with the topic of suicide all warrant a closer evaluation by a person trained in matters of psychopathology and suicide risk. **Suicidal thoughts accompanied by a specific plan of how the suicide might be enacted (e.g., using a gun, jumping off a building) are more ominous than non-specific suicidal thoughts, and always warrant a quick and serious response. Suicidal thoughts in a person using alcohol, illicit drugs, or prescription drugs without supervision is another sign of serious danger, whether or not that person is *abusing* alcohol or drugs.**

It is not always easy to explore the nature and extent of suicidal thoughts with a suicidal person. Some persons seem relieved to be asked about their suicidal thoughts and share their thinking freely. Others are reluctant to be frank, fearing what it might mean if they are perceived to have "mental problems." Others have a tendency to deny or minimize their distress, pushing away offers of help. To evaluate the extent of suicidal thinking, it is important to be persistent. The pastor should not let him/herself be pushed too far away, or pushed away for long.

"Loss of insight" is a common symptom of depressive illness that is important to keep in mind. Depressed persons are often the last ones to realize the extent of their symptoms or impairment. They may believe that they have "always felt this way." They may have a plausible explanation for their symptoms or impairment (e.g., work pressures, marital problems). But the point is that depressed persons don't always realize that they are ill, they sometimes under-estimate the degree to which their illness affects them, and they are often quick to provide "legitimate reasons" for why it is reasonable to feel so miserable.

In truth, there is no simple or direct correlation between how a person looks on the outside (e.g., smiling, acting normally, able to do his/her work) and the severity of depression. Many men and women with severe depressive illness continue to work without showing their suffering. Some people have the ability to smile politely, engage in pleasant small-talk, and do a good job at work — repairing cars, arguing cases in court, closing real estate deals, or preaching sermons — through periods of suicidal anguish.

To make matters more complicated, there is a common tendency to believe that if the life problems pressing on a suicidal person are objective, serious, and visible for all to see (e.g., marital problems, work problems), there is no need to consider a psychiatric diagnosis or worry about *serious* suicide risk. There is a common tendency to believe that situational crises will resolve themselves over time, so that psychiatric consultations are really unnecessary in these cases. Though situational crises seem more benign than those suicidal crises with no apparent explanation, it is important to understand that many people die by suicide in the throes of transient, situational stress. The fact that a suicidal crisis seems "justified by the circumstances" should *never* lead the pastor to assume there is little risk of death, or to relax his/her vigilance.

If some severely suicidal persons don't look too depressed, and if others deny they are depressed or refuse offers of help, how is a concerned relative, friend, or clergyperson supposed to recognize suicide risk? Sometimes we can't know. Sometimes we have to make educated guesses. In ambiguous situations, where one has a suspicion that something is wrong but can't be sure, one useful strategy is to meet informally with several family members or close friends to compare notes and enlist their help in deciding whether the pastor's concerns are well-founded. This kind of meeting is not the same as "going behind a person's back" — it is an expression of loving concern.

The presence of a psychiatric disorder should always increase concern about suicide risk. Studies of large, unselected groups of persons who died by suicide consistently show that more than 95% of all deaths by suicide occur in the context of a major psychiatric illness — most often major depression, alcoholism, drug abuse, or schizophrenia (Clark and Horton-Deutsch, 1992). At least half of all suicide victims were not aware they had a psychiatric disorder and were not in mental health treatment at the time. These patterns seem to apply to all age groups (i.e., adolescent, young adult, middle-aged, and elderly suicides) equally well.

Most persons afflicted with major depression, alcoholism, drug abuse, and schizophrenia do *not* die by suicide, so it is not fair to think that these illnesses "cause" suicide by themselves in the absence of other contributing circumstances. But there is no question that these illnesses betoken a *markedly increased risk of death by suicide*. Fifteen percent of persons experiencing major depression, ten percent of those experiencing schizophrenia, and four percent abusing alcohol eventually die by suicide. **Thus all persons who express suicidal ideas while exhibiting symptoms of depression, alcohol abuse, drug abuse, or schizophrenia should be evaluated promptly by a qualified mental health professional.**

Helping the suicidal person access treatment

If a troubled person admits to suicidal thoughts, or if the pastor has a strong suspicion of suicidal symptoms, the pastor should recommend an evaluation by a mental health professional. This recommendation should be repeated firmly and directly to the subject's family members. Many people are reluctant to hear or accept a recommendation to consult with a mental health professional for a variety of reasons. They may feel comfortable talking with the clergyperson, but do not want to consult an unfamiliar professional. They may interpret the recommendation as an insult to their mental competence. They may not "believe in" or trust mental health professionals — many people don't. They may think the recommendation will lead to burdensome expenses. They may fear that the recommendation will culminate in an unwanted involuntary hospitalization.

The clergyperson's job in this situation is to emphasize the necessity of a prompt evaluation and to address any hesitancies or reservations. It is not enough to make a referral and then wash one's hands of the matter, because many laypersons do not understand the gravity of suicide risk, nor do they understand how to access mental health care. In this sense suicidal symptoms can be compared to a bad leg injury, where it is necessary to visit a doctor quickly for an x-ray to determine whether or not the limb is broken. If broken, the fracture must be repaired promptly or permanent damage will result. Suicidal ideation is no less serious a symptom. Most people would *insist* that a family member or friend see a doctor right away for a serious leg injury, but — unfortunately — the same is not true for suicidal thoughts.

A qualified mental health professional should be willing to meet with the symptomatic person and family members within a very short period of time to assess the situation, and should be prepared to render an opinion in plain English after one or more visits. The professional should discuss sensible treatment options, their cost in terms of time and money, and the risk of foregoing treatment. The final decisions about whether to pursue treatment, what kind of treatment to pursue, and choice of therapist always rests with the patient and the patient's family, except in the rare circumstance when immediate hospitalization is deemed necessary to protect the patient from his/her own suicidal impulses.

It will be easier to make a firm and convincing referral if the pastor has had positive experiences with mental health professionals in the past — but not everyone has. How can a pastor make a referral with confidence if he/she is not familiar with the mental health services available locally, or if he/she doesn't know how to identify someone specializing in matters of suicide risk? There are a number of options. One could call the local medical society and ask for the names of psychiatrists who evaluate suicidal persons. One could suggest that the family discuss the matter with their family physician, who will ordinarily know mental health professionals that he/she can recommend. One could contact several different mental health professionals in the community and ask each the same question: Who in the community is particularly good at evaluating suicide risk and making appropriate treatment plans? When the same name is recommended by several different professionals, there is a greater likelihood that the mentioned person has the desired competencies.

Most psychiatrists and some — but not all — social workers, psychologists, and pastoral counselors have the necessary background and training to evaluate suicide risk and implement treatment. It may require some diligence and effort to find qualified professional help. It is generally best for children and adolescents to be referred to someone who specializes in child/adolescent services, and for the elderly to be referred to someone who specializes in geriatric services.

Recommended for Further Reading

Berman AL (editor): *Suicide Prevention: Case Consultations.* New York, Springer, 1990.

Berman AL, Jobes DA: *Adolescent Suicide: Assessment and Intervention.* Washington, DC, American Psychological Association Press, 1991.

Blumenthal SJ, Kupfer DJ (editors): *Suicide over the Life Cycle.* Washington, DC, American Psychiatric Press, Inc., 1990.

Bongar B (editor): *Suicide: Guidelines for Assessment, Management, and Treatment.* New York, Oxford University Press, 1992.

Leenaars A, Wenckstern S (editors): *Suicide Prevention in Schools.* Washington, D.C., Hemisphere, 1990.

Maris R, Berman AL, Maltsberger JT, Yufit R (editors): *Assessment and Prediction of Suicide.* New York, Guilford Press, 1992.

Osgood N: *Suicide in Later Life.* New York, Lexington, 1992.

Roy A (editor): *Suicide.* Baltimore, Williams & Wilkins, 1986.

Styron W: *Darkness Visible: A Memoir of Madness.* New York, Random House, 1990.

Wertheimer A: *A Special Scar: The Experiences of People Bereaved by Suicide.* New York, Routledge, 1991.

References

Brent D, Perper JA, Allman CJ, Moritz GM, Wartella MF, Zelenak JP: The presence and accessibility of firearms in the homes of adolescent suicides: A case-control study. *Journal of the American Medical Association* 266: 2989-2995, 1991.

Centers for Disease Control: Attempted suicide among high school students — United States, 1990. *Morbidity and Mortality Weekly Report* 40: 633-635, 1991.

Clark DC, Horton-Deutsch SL: Assessment *in Absentia*: The Value of the psychological autopsy method for studying antecedents of suicide and predicting future suicides. In Maris RW, Berman AL, Maltsberger JT, Yufit RI (editors): *Assessment and Prediction of Suicide.* New York, Guilford Press, 1992, pages 144-182.

Kashani JH, Goddard P, Reid JC: Correlates of suicidal ideation in a community sample of children and adolescents. *Journal of the American Academy of Child and Adolescent Psychiatry* 28: 912-917, 1989.

Meehan PJ, Lamb JA, Saltzman LE, O'Carroll PW: Attempted suicide among young adults: Progress toward a meaningful estimate of prevalence. *American Journal of Psychiatry* 149: 41-44, 1992.

Moscicki EK, O'Carroll P, Rae DS, Locke BZ, Roy A, Regier DA: Suicide attempts in the Epidemiological Catchment Area Study. *Yale Journal of Biology and Medicine* 61: 259-268, 1988.

Petronis KR, Samuels JF, Moscicki EK, Anthony JC: An epidemiologic investigation of potential risk factors for suicide attempts. *Social Psychiatry and Psychiatric Epidemiology* 25: 193-199, 1990.

Walker M, Moreau D, Weissman MM: Parents' awareness of children's suicide attempts. *American Journal of Psychiatry* 147: 1364-1366, 1990.

Appendix B

CDC Recommendations for a Community Plan for the Prevention and Containment of Suicide Clusters

Division of Injury Epidemiology and Control
Center for Environmental Health and Injury Control
Centers for Disease Control
Atlanta, Georgia 30333

Prepared by
Patrick W. O'Carroll, M.D., M.P.H.
James A. Mercy, Ph.D.
John A. Steward, M.P.H.

Original citation:
Centers for Disease Control. CDC recommendations for a community plan for the prevention and containment of suicide clusters. *Morbidity and Mortality Weekly Report* 37 (suppl. no. S-6): 1-12, 1988.

Introduction

Recent suicide clusters among teenagers and young adults have received national attention, and public concern about this issue is growing. Unfortunately, our understanding of the causes and means of preventing suicide clusters is far from complete. A suicide cluster may be defined as a group of suicides or suicide attempts, or both, that occur closer together in time and space than would normally be expected in a given community. A statistical analysis of national mortality data indicates that clusters of completed suicide occur predominantly among adolescents and young adults, and that such clusters account for approximately 1%–5% of all suicides in this age group (1). Suicide clusters are thought by many to occur through a process of "contagion," but this hypothesis has not yet been formally tested (2,3). Nevertheless a great deal of anecdotal evidence suggests that, in any given suicide cluster, suicides occurring later in the cluster often appear to have been influenced by suicides occurring earlier in the cluster. Ecologic evidence also suggests that exposure of the general population to suicide through television may increase the risk of suicide for certain susceptible individuals (4,5), although this effect has not been found in all studies (6,7).

The Centers for Disease Control (CDC) have assisted several state and local health departments in investigating and responding to apparent clusters of suicide and suicide attempts. These clusters created a crisis atmosphere in the communities in which they occurred and engendered intense concern on the part of parents, students, school officials, and others. In the midst of these clusters of suicides or suicide attempts, community leaders were faced with the simultaneous tasks of trying to prevent the cluster from expanding and trying to manage the crisis that already existed. Potential opportunities for prevention were often missed during the early stages of response as community leaders searched for information on how best to respond to suicide clusters.

The recommendations contained in this report were developed to assist community leaders in public health, mental health, education, and other fields to develop a community response plan for suicide clusters or for situations that might develop into suicide clusters. A workshop for developing these recommendations was jointly sponsored by the New Jersey State Department of Health and CDC on November 16–17, 1987, in Newark, New Jersey. Participants in that workshop included persons who had played key roles in community responses to nine different suicide clusters. They were from a variety of different sectors including education, medicine, local government, community mental health, local crisis centers, and state public health and mental health. Also participating in this workshop were representatives from the National Institute of Mental Health (NIMH), the Indian Health Service (IHS), the American Association of Suicidology (AAS), and the Association of State and Territorial Health Officials (ASTHO).

These recommendations should not be considered explicit instructions to be followed by every community in the event of a suicide cluster. Rather, they are meant to provide community leaders with a conceptual framework for developing their own suicide-cluster-response plans, adapted to the particular needs, resources, and cultural characteristics of their communities. These recommendations will be revised periodically to reflect new knowledge in the field of suicide prevention and experience acquired in using this plan.

Certain elements of the proposed plan for the prevention and containment of suicide clusters are quite different from those of crisis-response plans for other community emergencies. These differences are primarily attributable to the potentially contagious nature of suicidal behavior and to the stigma and guilt often associated with suicide. Other elements of the proposed plan, however, are germane to crisis-response plans in general. Therefore, state and local health planners might consider whether the plan they develop from these recommendations should be integrated into existing guidelines for managing other emergencies or mental health crises.

I. **A community should review these recommendations and develop its own response plan before the onset of a suicide cluster.**

Comment. When a suicide cluster is occurring in a community — or when such a cluster seems about to occur —several steps in our recommended response plan should be taken right away. If such a timely reaction is to be possible, the response plan must necessarily already be developed, agreed upon, and understood by all the participants at the onset of the crisis. The recommended response requires a great deal of coordination among various sectors of the community. Such coordination is sometimes difficult to establish at the best of times and may be even more difficult to establish in the face of a crisis.

In the early days of an evolving suicide cluster there has typically been a great deal of confusion. There is often a sense of urgency in the community that something needs to be done to prevent additional suicides, but there has usually been little initial coordination of effort in this regard. Moreover, community members often disagree about precisely what should be done to prevent a cluster from expanding. In almost every case, communities ultimately develop some sort of plan for responding to the crisis in a coordinated manner, but opportunities for prevention are often missed in the crucial first hours of the response.

II. The response to the crisis should involve all concerned sectors of the community and should be coordinated as follows:

A. Individuals from concerned agencies — education, public health, mental health, local government, suicide crisis centers, and other appropriate agencies — should be designated to serve on a coordinating committee, which would be responsible for deciding when the response plan should be implemented and coordinating its implementation.

B. One agency should be designated as the "host" agency for the plan. The individual representing that agency would have the following responsibilities:

1. Call the initial meeting of the coordinating committee before any crisis occurs so that these recommendations can be incorporated into a plan that reflects the particular resources and needs of the community (see Section III, below).

2. Establish a notification mechanism by which the agency would be made aware of a potentially evolving suicide cluster (see Comment, below).

3. Convene the coordinating committee when it appears that a suicide cluster is occurring, or when it is suspected that a cluster may occur due to the influence of one or more recent suicides or other traumatic deaths (see Section IV, below). At this initial meeting, the members of the coordinating committee could decide whether to implement the community response plan and how extensive the response needs to be.
4. Maintain the suicide-cluster-response plan. The coordinating committee should meet periodically to assure that the plan remains operational.
5. Revise the community plan periodically to reflect new knowledge in the field of suicide prevention, the community's experiences in using the plan, and changes in the community itself.

Comment. Every effort should be made to promote and implement the proposed plan as a community endeavor. During past suicide clusters, a single agency has often found itself "in the hot seat," that is, as the focal point of demands that something be done to contain the suicide cluster. No single agency, however, has the resources or expertise to adequately respond to an evolving suicide cluster. Moreover, the emergence of one agency as the sole focus for responding to an apparent suicide cluster has several unfortunate consequences. The agency and its representatives run the danger of becoming scapegoats for a community's fear and anger over the apparent cluster. Such a focus can potentially blind a community to other valuable resources for responding to the crisis and to basic community problems that may have engendered the crisis.

The concept of a "host" agency was developed because — even though the response will involve a variety of different agencies and community groups — one person must necessarily take responsibility for establishing a notification mechanism, maintaining the response plan, and calling meetings of the coordinating committee as outlined above. Which agency should serve as the host agency should be decided by each community. In past clusters, for example, a school district, a municipal government, a mental health association, and even a private, nonprofit mental health center have taken the lead in organizing their community's response. State or local public health or mental health agencies might also serve as host agencies for the plan. The role of host agency might also be rotated among the various agencies represented on the coordinating committee.

The notification mechanism by which the host agency would be made aware of a potentially evolving suicide cluster would vary from community to community. In small communities, one death of a teenager by suicide might be unusual, and information about the death would be quickly transmitted to a county-level host agency. In some large communities, however, there are many suicides each year among young persons. Clearly, a more formal system would be needed in such a county to notify the host agency when an unusual number of suicides had occurred in a particular high school or municipality.

Determining whether to implement the response plan is not an all-or-nothing decision. Indeed, an important function of the coordinating committee is to decide to what extent the plan will be implemented. In situations in which it is feared that a cluster of suicides may be about to start, for example, the implementation of the plan might be quite subtle and limited, whereas in the event of a full-blown community crisis the implementation should be more extensive.

III. The relevant community resources should be identified.

In addition to the agencies represented on the coordinating committee, the community should also seek to identify and enlist help from other community resources, including (but not limited to):

a) hospitals and emergency departments
b) emergency medical services
c) local academic resources
d) clergy
e) parents groups (e.g., PTA)
f) suicide crisis centers/hotlines

g) survivor groups
h) students
i) police
j) media
k) representatives of education, public health, mental health, and local government, if not already represented on the coordinating committee

Comment. The roles of each of the above groups should be defined as clearly as possible in the response plan before any crisis occurs. These roles should be agreed upon and reviewed by persons representing those groups. Most of those involved in the response will already know how to perform their particular duties. However, appropriate training for the staff of these groups should be provided as necessary (8). For example, if it is deemed desirable to conduct surveillance for suicide attempts through hospital emergency departments, officials at the state or local public health department might help design the system and train the emergency department staff. Other potential resources for training and counseling include state and local mental health agencies, mental health and other professional associations, and suicide crisis centers.

It is particularly important that representatives of the local media be included in developing the plan. In at least one community faced with a suicide cluster, the media collaborated in preparing voluntary guidelines for reporting suicide clusters. Although frequently perceived to be part of the problem, the media can be part of the solution. If representatives of the media are included in developing the plan, it is far more likely that their legitimate need for information can be satisfied without the sensationalism and confusion that has often been associated with suicide clusters.

The following example representing a composite of several actual suicide clusters illustrates the need for inclusion of and cooperation among many community organizations. Suppose that two high school students from the same school commit suicide in separate incidents on a weekend during the regular school year. The coordinating committee decides that these two deaths may increase the risk of suicide or attempted suicide among other students. The responsibilities of some of the relevant community resources might be as follows: School officials might be responsible for announcing the deaths to the students in an appropriate manner (discussed below, Section VI). School counselors and teachers might assist in identifying any students whom they think are at high risk; students in the school might also help in this regard. The local mental health agency might provide counselors to work with troubled students, as well as supply training and support for the teachers. Emergency departments of community hospitals might set up a suicide-attempt surveillance system that would increase the sensitivity with which suicide attempters were identified and would ensure proper referral of the attempters for counseling. Hotlines might help identify potential suicide attempters, and police might assist in locating such persons when appropriate. Police may also help by identifying and maintaining contact with such high-risk persons as high school dropouts and those with a history of delinquency. Local government or public health authorities might help coordinate these various efforts, if so designated by the coordinating committee.

IV. The response plan should be implemented under either of the following two conditions:

A. When a suicide cluster occurs in the community; that is, when suicides or attempted suicides occur closer together in space and time than is considered by members of the coordinating committee to be usual for their community; — OR —

B. When one or more deaths from trauma occur in the community (especially among adolescents or young adults) which the members of the coordinating committee think may potentially influence others to attempt or complete suicide.

Comment. It is difficult to define a "suicide cluster" explicitly. Clearly, both the number and the degree of "closeness" of cases of suicide in time and space that would constitute a suicide cluster vary depending on the size of the community and on its background incidence of suicide. But when a community considers that it is facing a cluster of suicides, it is essentially irrelevant whether the incident cases of suicide meet some predefined statistical test of significance. With the suddenly heightened awareness of and concern about suicide in such a community, steps should be taken to prevent further suicides that may be caused in part by the atmosphere, or "contagion," of the crisis.

In several clusters of suicides or suicide attempts, the crisis situation was preceded by one or more traumatic deaths—intentional or unintentional—among the youth of the community. For example, in the 9 months preceding one cluster of four suicides and two suicide attempts among persons 15–24 years of age, there were four traumatic deaths among persons in the same age group and community — two from unintentional injuries, one from suicide, and one of undetermined intentionality. One of the unintentional-injury deaths was caused by a fall from a cliff. Two of the persons who later committed suicide in the cluster had been close friends of this fall victim; one of the two had witnessed the fall.

The hypothesis that a traumatic death can kindle a suicide cluster regardless of whether it is caused by intentional or unintentional injuries has not yet been tested. Nevertheless, the available anecdotal evidence suggests that some degree of implementation of the response plan be considered when a potentially influential traumatic death occurs in the community — especially if the person who dies is an adolescent or young adult.

We should emphasize that the fear of a contagious effect of suicide is not the only reason to implement this plan. For example, suppose that in the wake of some local economic downturn a community noted an excess of suicide deaths among persons who had been laid off from work. This would be a suicide cluster, and it would be entirely appropriate for the coordinating committee to implement the response plan. It is irrelevant that the suicides are not apparently related to contagion from previous suicides but to a "common-source" problem, since there is an identified population (laid-off workers) potentially at a suddenly increased risk of suicide.

Whether and when to implement the response plan should be determined by the coordinating committee. At this stage of our understanding of suicide clusters, we cannot specify that the response plan should be implemented only under a particular list of circumstances. Until further scientific investigation and experience with suicide clusters provides us with a more empirical basis for deciding when to implement the response plan, we must rely on prudent judgments by community leaders regarding the potential for further suicides in their communities.

V. If the response plan is to be implemented, the first step should be to contact and prepare the various groups identified above.
   A. Immediately notify those who will play key roles in the crisis response of the deaths that prompted the implementation of the response plan (if they are not already aware of them).
   B. Review the respective responsibilities and tasks with each of these key players.
   C. Consider and prepare for the problems and stresses that these persons may encounter — burnout, feelings of guilt if new suicides occur, and the like — as they carry out their assigned tasks.

Comment. Timely preparation of the groups involved is critical. In a past cluster that began with a scenario similar to that described in Section III above, the teachers and the students both heard about the suicide deaths at the same time over the school loudspeaker. The teachers were entirely unprepared to deal with the emotional response of the students and did not know what to say to them or where to refer those who were most upset. It would have been far preferable to have called a pre-school meeting with the teachers to outline the problem, discuss the appropriate roles of the teachers, and announce the various resources that were available (9). Support staff at the school — secretaries, bus drivers, janitors, nurses, and others — might also have been included at the meeting. Such preparation could have been of enormous help in several past suicide clusters.

VI. The crisis response should be conducted in a manner that avoids glorifying the suicide victims and minimizes sensationalism.

A. Community spokespersons should present as accurate a picture as possible of the decedent(s) to students, parents, family, media, and others (see Section VIII, below).

B. If there are suicides among persons of school age, the deaths should be announced (if necessary) in a manner that will provide maximal support for the students while minimizing the likelihood of hysteria.

Comment. Community spokespersons should avoid glorifying decedents or sensationalizing their deaths in any way (9). To do so might increase the likelihood that someone who identifies with the decedents or who is having suicidal thoughts will also attempt suicide, so as to be similarly glorified or to receive similar positive attention. One community that had several suicides among high school students installed a "memorial bench" on the school grounds, with the names of the suicide victims engraved on the bench. Although this gesture was undoubtedly intended to demonstrate sincere compassion, such a practice is potentially very dangerous.

Spokespersons should also avoid vilifying the decedents in an effort to decrease the degree to which others might identify with them. In addition to being needlessly cruel to the families of the decedents, such an approach may only serve to make those who do identify with the decedents feel isolated and friendless.

If the suicide victims are of school age, the deaths should be announced privately to those students who are most likely to be deeply affected by the tragedy — close friends, girl friends, boy friends, and the like. After the teachers are briefed (see Section V), the suicide deaths might be announced to the rest of the students either by individual teachers or over the school loudspeaker when all the students are in homeroom or some other similarly small, supervised groups. Funeral services should not be allowed to unnecessarily disrupt the regular school schedule.

VII. Persons who may be at high risk should be identified and have at least one screening interview with a trained counselor; these persons should be referred for further counseling or other services as needed.

  A. Active measures:
    1. Identify relatives (siblings, parents, children) of the decedents and provide an opportunity for them to express their feelings and to discuss their own thoughts about suicide with a trained counselor.
    2. Similarly, identify and provide counseling for boy friends/girl friends, close friends, and fellow employees who may be particularly affected by the deaths.
      a) Strategies to identify associates of the decedents or others who may be at increased risk of suicide might include: identifying the pall bearers at the funeral services of the decedent(s); checking with the funeral director regarding visitors who seemed particularly troubled at the services; keeping a list of hospital visitors of suicide attempters; and verifying the status of school absentees in the days following the suicide of a student.
    3. In the case of suicides among school-age persons, enlist the aid of teachers and students in identifying any students whom they think may be at increased risk of suicide.
    4. Identify and refer past and present suicide attempters for counseling if these persons were substantially exposed to suicide (see below), regardless of whether they were close friends of the decedents.
      a) "Substantially exposed" persons would include, for example, students in the same high school or workers at the same job location as the suicide victims. In past suicide clusters, such persons have committed or attempted suicide even though they did not personally know the victims who had committed suicide earlier in the cluster.
    5. Identify and refer persons with a history of depression or other mental illness or with concurrent mental illness who were substantially exposed to suicide (see Section VII.A.4.a, above).

6. Identify and refer persons whose social support may be weakest and who have been substantially exposed to suicide. Examples of such persons include:
   a) students who have recently moved into the school district
   b) students who come from a troubled family
   c) persons who have been recently widowed or divorced, or who have recently lost their jobs.

B. Passive measures:
   1. Consider establishing hotlines or walk-in suicide crisis centers — even temporarily — if they do not already exist in the community; announce the availability of such hotlines/centers.
   2. Provide counselors at a particular site (such as school, church, community center) and announce their availability for anyone troubled by the recent deaths.
      a) If suicides have occurred among school-age persons, provide counselors in the schools if possible; announce their availability to the students.
   3. Enlist the local media to publish sources of help — hotlines, walk-in centers, community meetings, and other similar sources.
   4. Make counseling services available to persons involved in responding to the crisis as well.

Comment. The recommendations for active measures to identify persons at high risk of suicide are based largely on scientific evidence that certain factors increase the risk of suicide. For example, mental illness (especially depressive illness) (10) and a history of past suicide attempts (11) are both strong risk factors for suicide. Certain sociologic factors such as unemployment (12), being widowed or divorced (13,14), other bereavement (15,16), and mobility (17), also appear to be important risk factors for suicide.

The role of imitation or "contagion" is, as we noted above, less well-established than the risk factors listed above. Nevertheless, the anecdotal evidence from suicide clusters is quite compelling, and several of the specific suggestions made above regarding who should be considered for screening are based on such evidence. For example, in one high school-based cluster, two persons who committed suicide late in the cluster had been pall bearers at the funerals of suicide victims who had died earlier in the cluster. It is likely that persons who are exposed to one or more of the aforementioned risk factors — depression or recent loss, for example — may be more susceptible to a contagious effect of suicide.

VIII. A timely flow of accurate, appropriate information should be provided to the media.

A. Make certain that a single account of the situation is presented by appointing one person as information coordinator. This person's duties would include:
   1. meeting frequently with designated media spokespersons (see Section VIII. B, below) to share news and information, and to make certain that the spokespersons share a common understanding of the current situation
   2. "directing traffic" — referring requests for particular types of information to selected media spokespersons or to others (e.g., academic resources)
   3. maintaining a list of local and national resources for appropriate referral of media inquiries
   4. scheduling and holding press conferences.
B. Appoint a single media spokesperson from each of the relevant community sectors — public health, education, mental health, local government, and the like.
   1. Each sector represented on the coordinating committee should have a spokesperson. This person is not necessarily the same representative who serves on the coordinating committee.
   2. Spokespersons from additional agencies or public groups may be designated as appropriate.
C. These spokespersons should provide frequent, timely access to the media and present a complete and honest picture of the pertinent events. When appropriate, regularly scheduled press conferences should be held.
   1. Avoid "whitewashing" — that is, saying that everything is under control or giving other assurances that may later

prove unwarranted. This practice would undermine the credibility of the community spokespersons.

2. Discuss the positive steps being taken, and try to get the media to help in the response by reporting where troubled persons can go for help.

D. The precise nature of the methods used by decedent(s) in committing suicide should not be disclosed. For example, it is accurate to state that an individual committed suicide by carbon monoxide poisoning. But it is not necessary — and is potentially very dangerous — to explain that the decedent acquired a hose from a hardware store, that s/he hooked it up to the tail pipe of a car, and then sat in a car with its engine running in a closed garage at a particular address. Such revelations can only make imitative suicides more likely and are unnecessary to a presentation of the manner of death.

E. Enlist the support of the community in referring all requests for information to these spokespersons.

Comment. If some suicide clusters spread through "contagion," the vehicle for such contagion is information, perhaps sensationalized information, about the suicides that have occurred. The role of the media in causing or exacerbating a suicide cluster is controversial, but some investigators will no longer even discuss an evolving suicide cluster with media representatives for fear that newspaper or television accounts will lead to further suicides. Although a definitive understanding of this issue must be left to future research, it is prudent in the meantime to try to prevent needlessly sensationalized or distorted accounts of evolving suicide clusters.

The media spokespersons should meet as a group and with the information coordinator regularly; under certain circumstances, they may need to check with each other several times a day. Gaining the cooperation of the community in referring requests to these spokespersons is a formidable task and will require early and ongoing efforts if it is to be accomplished. It may be helpful to assure community members that it is all right to say "no" to media phone calls or requests for interviews.

The cooperation of parents is especially essential in the context of a school-based suicide cluster. Interviews with students about the suicide of one or more of their peers can be very stressful. Parents who do not wish to have their children interviewed may be able to prevent such interviews by refusing to sign a release statement. A handout addressing how media requests should be handled might be prepared and distributed to parents, students, and other appropriate persons.

Gaining the cooperation of media representatives in this regard is also a formidable task. In the midst of a crisis, the frequent presentation of accurate and credible information is the best means of establishing such cooperation. It is preferable, however, to develop a working relationship with local media representatives before a crisis occurs.

IX. Elements in the environment that might increase the likelihood of further suicides or suicide attempts should be identified and changed.

Comment. If a particular method or site was used in previous suicides or suicide attempts, modification efforts should be addressed to these methods or sites first. For example, if the decedent(s) jumped off a particular building, bridge, or cliff, barriers might be erected to prevent other such attempts. If the decedent(s) committed suicide by carbon monoxide poisoning in a particular garage, access to that garage should be limited or monitored or both. If the decedent(s) committed suicide with a firearm or by taking an overdose of drugs, then restricting immediate access to firearms or to potentially lethal quantities of prescription drugs should be considered. In the case of suicides committed in jail, belts and other articles that may be used to commit suicide by hanging should be removed, and vigilance over the jail cells should be increased. Some of these modifications can be accomplished directly through the efforts of the coordinating committee, while others (limiting access to drugs or firearms) can only be suggested by the committee for others to consider.

Although immediate environmental modifications may be suggested by methods used in previous suicides, the modifications need not be limited only to those methods. If there is concern, for example, that the risk of suicide for particular adolescents may have been increased because of the influence of previous traumatic deaths, then common methods of suicide — firearm injury, carbon monoxide poisoning, overdose — should be made temporarily unavailable if possible. The coordinating committee should consider a variety of potentially relevant environmental factors in developing this element of the response strategy.

X. Long-term issues suggested by the nature of the suicide cluster should be addressed.

Comment. Common characteristics among the victims in a given suicide cluster may suggest that certain issues need to be addressed by the community. For example, if the decedent(s) in a particular suicide cluster tended to be adolescents or young adults who were outside the main stream of community life, efforts might be made to bring such persons back into the community. Or, if a large proportion of the suicide attempters or completers had not been suspected of having any problems, then a system should be developed (or the present system altered) so that troubled persons could receive help before they reached the stage of overt suicidal behavior.

Communities should consider establishing a surveillance system for suicide attempts as well as completed suicides. Suicide-attempt surveillance systems are almost nonexistent; yet the benefits of such systems are potentially great. In the context of a suicide cluster, such a system would allow persons who have attempted suicide in the past to be identified. Such persons are known to be at high risk of further suicide attempts. It would also allow for ongoing identification of high-risk persons during and after the current crisis. Communities should consider establishing suicide-attempt surveillance systems in their local emergency departments or wherever appropriate.

This plan should be modified according to the community's experience with its operation. Parts of the plan that have worked well in a given setting should be stressed in the updated plan, and parts that were inapplicable or that did not work should be excluded. Finally, the Centers for Disease Control requests that communities that use the plan notify us of their experiences with the plan to allow appropriate updating of this document. Please write to:

Chief, Intentional Injuries Section
Mailstop F-36
Centers for Disease Control
1600 Clifton Road NE
Atlanta, GA 30333

References

1. Gould MS, Wallenstein S, Kleinman M. A Study of time-space clustering of suicide. Final report. Atlanta, Georgia: Centers for Disease Control, September 1987; [contract no. RFP 200-85-0834].
2. Robbins D, Conroy C. A cluster of adolescent suicide attempts: is suicide contagious? *J Adolesc Health Care* 1983; 3: 253-5.
3. Davidson L, Gould MS. Contagion as a risk factor for youth suicide. In: *Report of the Secretary's Task Force on Youth Suicide, Vol. II: Risk factors for youth suicide.* Washington, DC: US Government Printing Office (1989).
4. Phillips DP, Carstensen LL. Clustering of teenage suicides after television news stories about suicide. *N Engl J Med* 1986; 315: 685-9.
5. Gould MS, Shaffer D. The impact of suicide in television movies: evidence of imitation. *N Engl J Med* 1986; 315: 690-4.
6. Phillips DP, Paight DJ. The impact of televised movies about suicide: a replicative study. *N Engl J Med* 1987; 317: 809-11.
7. Berman AL. Fictional suicide and imitative effects. *Am J Psychiatry 1988*; 145: 982-986.
8. Dunne EJ, McIntosh JL, Dunne-Maxim K, eds. *Suicide and its aftermath: understanding and counseling the survivors.* New York: WW Norton & Company, 1987: 151-182.
9. Lamb F, Dunne-Maxim K. Postvention in schools: policy and process. In: Dunne EJ, McIntosh JL, Dunne-Maxim K, eds. *Suicide and its aftermath: understanding and counseling the survivors.* New York: WW Norton & Company, 1987: 245-60.
10. Hagnell O, Lanke J, Rorsman B. Suicide rates in the Lundby study: mental illness as a risk factor for suicide. *Neuropsychobiology* 1981; 7: 248-53.

11. Paerregaard G. Suicide among attempted suicides: a 10-year follow-up. *Suicide* 1975; 5: 140-4.
12. Platt S. Suicidal behavior and unemployment: a literature review. In: Wescott G, Svensson P-G, Zollner HFK, eds. *Health policy implications of unemployment.* Copenhagen: World Health Organization, 1985: 87-132.
13. Monk M. Epidemiology of suicide. *Epidemiol Rev* 1987; 9: 51-69.
14. Smith JC, Mercy JA, Conn JM. Marital status and the risk of suicide. *Am J Public Health* 1988; 78: 78-80.
15. MacMahon B, Pugh TF. Suicide in the widowed. *Am J Epidemiol* 1965; 81: 23-31.
16. Bunch J, Barraclough B, Nelson B, et al. Suicide following bereavement of parents. *Soc Psychiatry* 1971; 6: 193-9.
17. South SJ. Metropolitan migration and social problems. *Social Science Quarterly* 1987; 68: 3-18.

Appendix C

Recommendations From a Workshop on Suicide Contagion and the Reporting of Suicide

March 1991

Sponsored by the Association of State and Territorial Health Officials and the New Jersey Department of Health

Funding provided by the Maternal and Child Health Bureau, Health Resources and Services Administration, U.S. Department of Health and Human Services

Introduction

Suicide among adolescents and young adults is a serious problem in the United States. In 1950, less than 6 percent of all suicides were committed by persons 15 to 24 years of age. By 1980, this proportion had grown to 20 percent of all suicides. The suicide rate among 15– to 24–year-olds increased nearly 300 percent during the period, from 4.5 per 100,000 in 1950 to more than 12 per

100,000 in 1980 (1). In 1987, the rate was 12.9 per 100,000, and suicide was the third leading cause of death in this age group (2). Today, only motor vehicle crashes surpass suicide as the leading cause of death among young persons 15 to 24 years old.

Youth suicide is a highly complex problem and clearly there are no simple solutions. Most youth suicides appear to be precipitated by some kind of stress such as getting into trouble, breaking up with a friend, school problems, or an argument with parents. However, these are normal stresses of adolescence and do not make the majority of young adults suicidal (3). To explain youth suicide, it is necessary to look beyond the apparent precipitant stressor. Scientific evidence supports the existence of a variety of risk factors, including biological markers (such as serotonin abnormalities and genetic effects), psychopathology and problem behaviors (depression, aggressiveness, antisocial behavior, and alcohol and drug abuse), and disturbed families (child abuse and/or other suicides in the family) (4). Suicide is the extreme outcome of a complex interplay of risk factors which together result in a young person taking his or her own life.

Several widely publicized reports of suicide clusters have stimulated interest in contagion as a potential component in the cause of youth suicide. A suicide cluster may be loosely defined as a group of suicides, suicide attempts, or both, that occur closer together than would normally be expected in a given community (5,6). Such clusters account for approximately 1 to 2 percent of all suicides among adolescents and young adults (7). Although cluster suicides have commanded recent attention, the phenomenon is not new. Historical accounts of such suicides can be traced back to ancient times (8). Serious study of the cluster phenomenon, however, began only in the early 1980s.

One mechanism thought to be involved in suicide contagion involves a combination of grief, identification, imitation, and highly charged emotional atmosphere that may engender a preoccupation with suicide among susceptible young people (6,8,9). Some susceptible persons may imitate the actions of those with whom they have developed a close personal relationship or understanding, whether real or imagined. If that individual should choose suicide as a method of dealing with life's problems, the susceptible young person may model the behavior, accepting that suicide is an appropriate method for dealing with painful or difficult problems in his or her life as well.

Although research results are not conclusive, some studies suggest that news accounts of real life suicides may trigger additional suicides. Newspaper and television accounts which seem to have the most powerful effects are those in which reporters and public officials appear to glamorize or romanticize a young person's suicide. See the two examples of news stories with high and low potential for contributing to suicide contagion at the end of this Appendix.

Public officials and media representatives should be aware of how their actions or statements might affect others in the community. They should also be aware of the various alternatives available for the presentation of news information. By working cooperatively, both public officials and news organizations can communicate information on a youth suicide in a way that has the lowest-possible risk of encouraging imitative behavior and that allows journalists to present newsworthy information.

Such cooperation among health and law enforcement officials, community leaders, media representatives, and suicidologists has frequently been recommended (6,10-12). In November 1989, the Association of State and Territorial Health Officials and the New Jersey Department of Health convened a meeting of suicidologists, public health officials, and news media representatives from around the country. Participants discussed methods of limiting the potential for suicide contagion without compromising the independence or integrity of any group represented at the meeting.

The participants' goal was not to develop community or journalistic standards, but rather to provide guidelines for public officials and the media to use when working with a suicide story. The participants recommended that the following core elements be considered in the process of reporting on youth suicide and preventing suicide clusters.

Recommendations

- **Suicide is often newsworthy—and will be reported.** It is the mission of a news organization to reflect what is happening in the community, and to convey true, accurate, and unbiased information to the public. Current editorial practice in many news organizations has been to report as suicide only those suicides that were committed in public, or by public officials. Other suicides are not reported as such, often at the request of the family of the deceased. Such selective reporting may suggest that only successful or important people commit suicide, and that suicide is an acceptable way to become recognized as a successful person.
- **"No comment" is not a productive response to a reporter covering a suicide story.** Withholding information from a reporter does not prevent coverage of a suicide, it only eliminates an opportunity to influence what is contained in that story. However, such a response may create or exacerbate an adversarial relationship between that individual (or organization) and the news media. Public officials should not feel obligated to provide an immediate answer to difficult questions. However, they should be prepared to provide a reasonable timetable for giving such answers, or be able to direct reporters to someone who can provide the answers.
- **Public officials and news reporters should take time to think about what is to be said or reported.** Impromptu, off-the-cuff comments by a public official may create or drive unfortunate coverage, and insensitive or incomplete news stories written under a short deadline may alienate public officials. Reporters and public officials should take time to present as accurate and complete a report as possible in language that is easy for the average citizen to understand. When appropriate, officials and reporters should agree to meet in comfortable surroundings where story details can be provided and major story points can be discussed. Dialogue should be encouraged between public officials and the media over points of concern in a suicide story. However, neither side should attempt to dictate what is to be reported.

- **A news story should not oversimplify the cause of a suicide.** A suicide is not the result of a single factor, but a complex interplay of many factors. Both public officials and news reporters should take care to explain that the final precipitating event was not the only cause of the suicide. Virtually all suicide victims have had a long history of problems, all of which contributed to the final event. It is not necessary to catalogue all the problems associated with an individual's suicide, but their existence should be acknowledged.
- **Extensive or prominent news coverage of a suicide event may contribute to suicide contagion in susceptible individuals.** Repetitive, ongoing coverage of a suicide event, or prominent front page coverage, may cause a suicide to become more impressive in the mind of a susceptible individual, and thus more attractive as a solution to his or her own problems. Both public officials and news reporters should discuss options to address this potential problem.
- **Both public officials and reporters should guard against sensationalizing the news coverage.** Lurid descriptions of the suicide, Romeo and Juliet comparisons, or rumors of suicide pacts may exacerbate the emotional atmosphere surrounding a suicide. The events surrounding a suicide should be reported in an objective, factual, and neutral manner, avoiding embellishments which may add to the emotional atmosphere.
- **News coverage that glorifies the victim or awards the victim celebrity status should be discouraged.** Public eulogies, flags at half-staff, and establishing permanent memorials may suggest to susceptible individuals that society is honoring the victim's act of suicide, rather than mourning the loss of the person.
- **Providing specific details on how the suicide occurred may be harmful.** A detailed description of the suicide method could be used as a "how-to" manual by persons contemplating suicide. This does not mean that general information about the method used should not be reported, but information such as the type of hose used, where it was purchased, and how it was hooked up to the exhaust, should be avoided.
- **Suicide should not appear to be a rewarding experience, or an appropriate or effective tool to achieve personal gain.** A sui-

cide death should never be described as a "successful" suicide. Both public officials and news reporters should make an effort to ensure that they do not present suicide as an appropriate means to deal with the break-up of a friendship, to retaliate against parental discipline, to avoid the shame of a failing grade, or to end suffering.

- **Risk factors for teenage suicide should be presented carefully and thoughtfully.** It should be clearly presented that there are many risk factors for suicide, not just one or two, and that it is normal for many individuals to experience one or more of these risk factors and to not be suicidal. A teenage suicide is the result of a complex interplay of many risk factors all of which contributed to the youth taking his or her own life.
- **A suicide is stressful not only to members of the family and other survivors, but to the community as well.** Including in a news report factual information on the risk factors for suicide, methods for identifying persons at high risk, and ways to prevent suicide can be very helpful. Many of these resources are already available within the community, such as adequately trained mental health professionals and suicide prevention centers.

References

1. U.S. Department of Health and Human Services, Public Health Service, Centers for Disease Control, *Youth Suicide in the United States, 1970-1980.* U.S. Government Printing Office, Washington, DC: 1986.
2. U.S. Department of Health and Human Services, Public Health Service, Centers for Disease Control, National Center for Health Statistics, *Vital Statistics of the United States, 1987. Vol. 2 - Mortality Part A.* Hyattsville, Maryland: 1989.
3. Shaffer, D., et al., Strategies for Prevention of Youth Suicide. *Public Health Reports,* 1987; 102:611-613.
4. Shaffer, D., et al., Preventing Teenage Suicide: A Critical Review. *Journal of the American Academy of Child and Adolescent Psychiatry,* 1988, 27, 6:675-687.
5. O'Carroll, P.W., Responding to Community-Identified Suicide Clusters: Statistical Verification of the Cluster is not the Primary Issue. *American Journal of Epidemiology,* 1990.

6. U.S. Department of Health and Human Services, Public Health Service, Centers for Disease Control, CDC Recommendations for a Community Plan for the Prevention and Containment of Suicide Clusters. *Morbidity and Mortality Weekly Report*, 1988; 37(S-6):1.
7. Gould, M.S., Wallenstein, S., Kleinman, M., Time-Space Clustering of Teenage Suicide. *American Journal of Epidemiology*, 1990; 131:71-78.
8. Davidson, L., Gould, M.S., Contagion as a Risk Factor for Youth Suicide. In: *Report of the Secretary's Task Force on Youth Suicide, Vol. 2: Risk Factors for Youth Suicide.* DHHS Pub. No. (ADM)89-1622. Washington, DC: Superintendent of Documents, U.S. Government Printing Office, 1989.
9. Robbins, D., Conroy, C., A Cluster of Adolescent Suicide Attempts: Is Suicide Contagious? *Journal of Adolescent Health Care*, 1983; 3:253-5.
10. Alcohol, Drug Abuse, and Mental Health Administration, *Report of the Secretary's Task Force on Youth Suicide, Vol. 1: Overview and Recommendations.* DHHS Pub. No. (ADM)89-1621. Washington, DC: Superintendent of Documents, U.S. Government Printing Office, 1989.
11. Berman, A.L., Interventions in the Media and Entertainment Sectors to Prevent Suicide. In: *Report of the Secretary's Task Force on Youth Suicide, Vol. IV: Strategies for the Prevention of Youth Suicide.* Washington, DC: Superintendent of Documents, U.S. Government Printing Office, 1989.
12. Gould, M.S., Suicide Contagion Among Adolescents. Testimony before the (New York) Senate Standing Committee on Mental Hygiene. February 10, 1988.

Examples of News Stories With High and Low Potential for Contagion

Example A

Story with High Potential for Suicide Contagion

Hundreds turned out at St. Joseph Church Monday for the funeral of Ralph Jones, 15, who shot himself in the head late Friday with his father's hunting rifle. Town Moderator Richard Lewis, along with State Senator Timothy Wells and Selectman's Chairman Marvin Brown, were among the many well-known people who offered their condolences to the sobbing Mary and Gavin Jones, the parents of the Jonestown High School sophomore.

Although no one could say for sure why Jones killed himself, classmates who didn't want to be quoted said Jones' girlfriend, Cynthia Luellen, also a sophomore at the high school, and Jones had been having difficulty. Jones, who had a large collection of comic books that his classmates admired, recently threw away most of the comics, which he'd collected over the last five or six years. Friends said he took them to the Jonestown dump and watched with tears in his eyes while the comics burned.

School closed at noon Monday and buses were on hand to transport those who wished to attend Jones' funeral. School officials said almost all of the student body of 1,200 attended. Flags in town were flown at half staff in his honor.

Police Chief Oscar Buster said Jones fired his father's rifle twice. "He must have missed the first time," Chief Buster speculated. "We're still looking for the missing bullet. And of course we found the second one."

Jones was born in Gunderson, Vermont, and moved to this town 10 years ago with his parents and sister, Rachel, who was uncontrollable at her brother's funeral. In addition to his comic book collection, Jones was known by his friends for his large snake collection. He also was a good swimmer. He had been a Cub Scout some years ago, but when he failed to pass his final badge, he quit.

Members of the School Committee and the Board of Selectmen are working to erect a special flag pole in the turnaround in front of the high school in Jones' honor.

Example B

Story With Low Potential for Suicide Contagion

Ralph Jones, 15, of Maplewood Drive, died Friday from a self-inflicted gunshot wound. The son of Mary and Gavin Jones, Ralph Jones was a sophomore at Jonestown High School.

He had lived in Jonestown since he moved here 10 years ago from Gunderson, Vermont, where he was born. His funeral at St. Joseph Church was held Sunday. School counselors are available to any students who wish to talk about Jones' death.

In addition to his parents, Jones is survived by his sister, Rachel.

VIII. Contributors

Herbert Anderson, Ph.D. is a Lutheran pastor and Professor of Pastoral Theology at Catholic Theological Union in Chicago. He is widely respected in the area of grief studies and grief counseling.

Rev. Homer U. Ashby, Jr., Ph.D. is Professor of Pastoral Care at McCormick Theological Seminary, Chicago and a pastoral counselor.

Laurel Arthur Burton, Th.D. is Anderson Professor of Religion and Medicine at Rush-Presbyterian-St. Luke's Medical Center, where he teaches ethics in the Medical College, practices family therapy, and is a member of the Ethics Consultation Service.

Nancy U. Cairns, Ph.D. is a clinical psychologist with twelve years' experience working with children, adolescents, and adults with chronic, life-threatening illness. She has authored or co-authored a number of research papers on the psychological and social ramifications of childhood cancer. Her clinical experience includes services for families experiencing chronic medical or psychiatric illness, child abuse, domestic violence, and sexual abuse and misconduct. She currently teaches and directs the Master's Program at the Illinois School of Professional Psychology.

David C. Clark, Ph.D. is Associate Professor in the Departments of Psychiatry and Psychology at Rush-Presbyterian-St. Luke's Medical Center in Chicago, where he is also Director of the Center for Suicide Research and Prevention. Dr. Clark is Associate Editor of the journal *Suicide and Life-Threatening Behavior* and Senior Editor of the international journal *CRISIS*.

Rabbi Steven L. Denker, M.A.H.L. was Associate Rabbi of Temple Sholom, Chicago; is a lecturer and teacher and an adjunct Lecturer of Theology at Loyola University - Chicago.

George Fitchett, D.Min. is Associate Professor in the Department of Religion, Health, and Human Values at Rush-Presbyterian-St. Luke's Medical Center in Chicago and Director of Research and Spiritual Assessment in that department. He is a Supervisor of the Association of Clinical Pastoral Education, a

Fellow of the College of Chaplains, and a member of the American Association of Pastoral Counselors. He is also the author of *Assessing Spiritual Needs: A Guide for Caregivers* and *Spiritual Assessment: A Guide to Selected Resources*.

John A. Gallagher, Ph.D. is Director, Corporate Ethics for the Holy Cross Health System in South Bend, Indiana.

Rev. Lucille Sider Groh, Ph.D. is Executive Director of the Samaritan Pastoral Counseling Center in Evanston, Illinois. Dr. Groh is a pastoral counselor and a clinical psychologist.

Ira S. Halper, M.D. is an Assistant Professor of Psychiatry and Director of the Cognitive Therapy Program at Rush-Presbyterian-St. Luke's Medical Center. Dr. Halper has an interest in the integration of biological and psychological approaches to psychiatric disorders and in the interface between psychology and religion.

Rev. Eimo E. Hinrichs is the Chaplain and Director of Pastoral Services at the George A. Zeller Mental Health Center in Peoria, Illinois. As the survivors of the suicide of their 14-year-old daughter, he and his wife, Patricia, are co-facilitators of a survivors of suicide support group.

Paul C. Holinger, M.D. is Professor of Psychiatry at Rush-Presbyterian-St. Luke's Medical Center and is currently practicing psychiatry and psychoanalysis in Chicago.

Thomas Jobe, M.D. has been an emergency psychiatrist and head of outpatient psychiatry services at the University of Illinois at Chicago since 1979. He is currently Associate Director of the Neuropsychiatric Section in the Department of Psychiatry there.

John T. Maltsberger, M.D. is with the Boston Psychoanalytic Society and Institute, and a faculty member at McLean Hospital of Harvard University. Dr. Maltsberger is the author of a number of landmark scientific papers and monographs on the assessment and management of suicide risk, including the book *Suicide Risk: The Formulation of Clinical Judgment*.

Robert J. Marx has been the Rabbi of Congregation Hakafa in Glencoe, Illinois since 1984. He received his Ph.D. from Yale University and for many years has convened a group known as *Parents Who Have Lost a Child*.

James D. McHolland, Ph.D. has integrated the resources of religion and psychology for thirty years, especially as they may ameliorate depression. He emphasizes an appreciation of religious diversity in training of graduate students in clinical psychology. Dr. McHolland also serves as consultant to three pastoral counseling centers in the Chicago area.

George Polk, S.T.M., M.Div. is Vice President of Religion and Health at Bethany Hospital, Chicago and Pastoral Educator of the North Central Region at A.C.P.E. Inc.

Rev. Charles T. Rubey is Manager of the Catholic Charities Family and Parish Support Division and Founding Director of LOSS (Loving Outreach to Survivors of Suicide), a self-help support group for persons who have lost a family member by suicide which has served the Chicagoland area since 1979.

Rev. James H. Shackelford, Ph.D. is a Presbyterian pastor and Clinical Director at the Pastoral Counseling Center of Lutheran General Hospital in the Chicago area.

Dan G. Stauffacher, D.Min. is a local church pastor at First Congregational Church, United Church of Christ of Geneva, Illinois, who has been involved with the mental health system in outpatient and inpatient settings since 1972, in addition to his pastoral work. He is active in professional organizations at both the regional and national levels where he has presented papers on the role of clergy in various facets of the topic and suicide.